# A REASON TO
# RISE

# A REASON TO
# RISE

OVERCOME ADVERSITY AND AWAKEN YOUR POWER

NADINE MULLER

First published in 2024 by Dean Publishing
PO Box 119
Mt. Macedon, Victoria, 3441
Australia
deanpublishing.com

Copyright © Nadine Muller

All rights reserved. No part of this publication may be reproduced, stored in a retrieval system or transmitted in any way or by any means, electronic, mechanical, photocopying, recording or otherwise, without the prior written permission of the author and publisher.

Cataloguing-in-Publication Data
National Library of Australia
Title: A Reason To Rise — Overcome Adversity and Awaken Your Power
Edition: 1st edition
ISBN: 978-1-925452-87-7
Category: Self-help/personal growth

The stories and opinions in this book reflect the author's recollection of events and personal way of working. Some specific names, locations, and identifying characteristics have been changed to protect the privacy of those depicted. The book also contains some experiences of trauma and the reader should take care of their own mental and emotional health when engaging in stories or exercises that may be triggering for them. Always consult professional advice when required.

This book deals with personal growth and isn't a substitute for professional advice in relation to one's mental or physical health or psychological issues. The information provided in this book is designed to provide helpful information on the subjects discussed using the author's personal experiences.

This book is not meant to be used, nor should it be used, to diagnose or treat any physical, emotional, or psychological medical condition. This book is about making personal choices and being responsible for your actions and results. Always consult your own professional health expert for advice regarding your mental or emotional health.

The publisher and author are not responsible for any specific health or psychological needs and are not liable for any damages or negative consequences from any treatment, action, application, or preparation to any person reading or following the information in this book. References are provided for informational purposes only and do not constitute endorsement of any websites or other sources. References or quotes used are to provide hope or context for the reader and not to endorse any specific framework or modality.

Neither the publisher nor the individual author(s) shall be liable for any physical, psychological, emotional, financial, or commercial damages, including, but not limited to, special, incidental, consequential, or other damages. Our views and rights are the same: you are responsible for your own choices, actions, and results.

Dedicated to my boys Dane,
Madden, and Beckham—for
together being my guiding compass.

In loving memory of my dad and
my angel babies whose collective
light all shine on in our hearts
and across these pages.

# CONTENTS

Introduction: We All Have a Reason to Rise .................... ix

Chapter 1: The Rising ....................................................... 1

Chapter 2: The Most Powerful Decision of Your Life ........ 23

Chapter 3: It's All Self-Mastery, Really ............................. 61

Chapter 4: Take The Direct Path ...................................... 97

Chapter 5: Courage Is Your Compass ........................... 139

Chapter 6: The Dark and Light of Life ........................... 183

Chapter 7: Caregiving .................................................... 213

Chapter 8: The Next Evolution ....................................... 255

Testimonials .................................................................. 277

Acknowledgments ......................................................... 281

About the Author .......................................................... 283

Endnotes ....................................................................... 284

## INTRODUCTION

# WE ALL HAVE A REASON TO RISE

I once thought my life was such a mess that I'd need the Jaws of Life rescue tools to untangle the complicated cluster of shit it had become. It wasn't through lack of trying though. If trying your ass off was an Olympic sport, then I'd be a freakin' gold medalist. I was *always* trying. You see, I came from a family lineage of accomplished and decorated military people—toughness, grit, and getting out of treacherous problems was our jam. We kinda excelled at it.

My grandfather, my brother, countless family members, and I have all been long-standing military personnel. We suck it up and get shit done! It's a family trait. It was instilled into us early, and I never questioned it. Being a hardcore action taker during a crisis was what I knew and what was expected. I could commando roll out of most situations.

Despite my thirteen years of military training and my decade as a critical care emergency registered nurse, nothing prepared me for what was about to unfold.

You see, life dished out a destiny I wasn't expecting, and I soon discovered that being tough and sucking it up like a soldier didn't really help me reach my highest potential. It was helpful in some ways, but it certainly wasn't the master principle of wholehearted happiness and success. Don't you just love finding things out the hard way? *Not*.

I guess life was trying to show me what Einstein claimed back in 1926: "God does not play dice." What was occurring in my life was dismantling my old existence as I knew it (along with my identity, beliefs, and any shred of sanity I had left) and reassembling a new one. A new existence that was given to me by fate, but up to *me* to fulfill by choice.

I have now come to believe that we are all handed a perfect destiny, even if it appears to be less than ideal. But it's up to us to fulfill our highest potential!

Now that, of course, does not mean our life's purpose is straightforward or handed to us on a silver platter with cheese, crackers, and wine. It's often a gritty process of self-discovery.

Right now, you may be at a crossroads in your life. You may feel a deep knowing in your soul that you are here for a greater purpose. I believe that if you feel that inner knowing, then you are bang on! Life is always talking to you through signs and intuitions and knowings, yet we must learn the language of our soul and behave in alignment with its calling. We must rise to the destiny that's in our heart before we see evidence of its existence.

Often, we are called to a destiny that we don't feel prepared for or capable of fulfilling. But that's the juice of life. That's the limb we must climb out to so we can see the bigger vision.

Problems and conflicts arise when we don't listen to that inner truth, or we cloud it with useless mind chatter and self-doubt so we never fully hear its call.

Let me ask you a few straight-up questions.

- Are you ready to live the highest vision for your life?
- Can you feel a frustrated greatness inside (that sense that you are born to do great things but never get the chance to fulfill that greatness)?
- Do you intuitively know in your heart there's a purpose for you?
- Do you have a fire in your belly that's burning for more (you just need to figure out what that *more* is)?
- Do you need to rise above an obstacle or cycle of suffering?

My guess is that you're a woman (or man) of incredible strengths. You may even wear many hats all at once and find yourself trying to be everything to everyone (because you can, right?). You are a capable, multitalented powerhouse with amazing gifts to offer, but there's just a couple of little things stopping you from unleashing your full potential ... Perhaps you're too exhausted, or questioning your worth or abilities, or maybe you just need some genuine support. I bet you can sense that the universe has something magical in store for you. You just need some clarity and a nudge in the right direction to claim it fully.

Through my decade-plus of high performance leadership, management, coaching, and mentoring, I have discovered that some of the most remarkable humans on Earth do not even realize their true power. Many feel something electric pulsating within them, but most don't know how to harness it and unleash it into the world.

If that's you, then read on, 'cause we're about to go on a journey that I can guarantee will change the way you think, love, and live.

Now, you may be thinking, *How can you make such a bold and outrageous claim on the first few pages of this book? Isn't that a bit OTT, Nadine?* Well, NO. You see, I believe in every single word I'm writing. The insights I'm going to share and the stories I'm about to tell are all true and messy and magnificent. They have single-handedly turned my life around and transformed my mind, body, spirit, and soul. Furthermore, they've gone on to create extraordinary ripple effects for thousands of people, especially women and mothers, and also families.

You see, I am here to push an agenda. I make no apologies for it. I am here to encourage, support, and ignite countless women to claim their birthright—to live their authentic and ultimate life and stand in their full feminine power.

How do I know this is possible? Well, I went from thinking I was "meant to struggle" and "work to the bone" to realizing my potential and moving from financial pittance to running a multi-seven-figure purpose-led business. I went through a marriage crisis to a marriage breakthrough. We decided to sell our house, home and worldschool our kids, travel Australia and the world, and live our best lives on our terms with our family in tow.

No matter how we choose to live and adventure, I wake up every day with passion, power, and zest for life. I'm not saying this is what you should aim for! Your dreams are yours. These are mine, and it took me some time to figure out that my dreams were worth pursuing. Not only that, my dreams were also, in fact, possible.

This is not a rags-to-riches type of book. Nor am I here to preach or save the day. I'm not here to rescue you from the trenches of despair. That's a solo job. I'm here to show you all the ladders, climbing ropes, and even fucking rocket ships you have *inside* that can hoist (or perhaps blast) you out of the pits and catapult you to new life-changing heights of joy and success.

Now, I ain't gonna sugarcoat this whole "live your dreams" caper. It's fucking tough work. But it's so darn amazing to live your dreams that I can hardly breathe just writing about it. I had to claw my way through mountains of obstacles and learn how to master my mind and time. I had to face my inner shit and work through bucketloads of humbling crap. But what I can assure you is that it was all worth it. And it is worth it. Every single bit.

I changed careers; I changed my mindset, and I changed what I believed was possible for me. Now I pinch myself because I can't believe how amazing my life is. Of course, this massive transformation didn't happen because I'm special or have superheroine abilities. It happened because I found better ways of doing things. Better ways of thinking, believing, and living. I learned some simple self-mastery skills that flipped my conditioning and elevated me to new territory. It gave me an invitation to liberation … and I took it and ran with it.

Now I get the honor of helping women all over the world do the same. To live life wholeheartedly and unapologetically on their terms.

There's a powerful quote by Leslie Littlejohn that says, "Be the woman who fixes another woman's crown without telling the world that it is crooked." And that's what we do. We have a beautiful tribe of supportive women fixing each other's crowns and living brave and bold lives.

So, if you're ready to kiss goodbye a disempowering mindset and harness a new way of believing and thinking … then this book is for you!

But don't worry, you're not taking this journey alone. You have a tribe of crown fixers and polishers who have your back! And I'm one of them.

Where you start doesn't have to be where you finish. I can guarantee that after you read my book and do the exercises, you *will* be in a different place from where you started. You will be more awake, more aware, and more empowered than before. And by doing the inner work, you will see results in the outer realm. Things will change! And not because of the "things" themselves but as a result of your inner transformation.

Trailblazing philosopher Dr Carl Jung said, "People will do anything, no matter how absurd, in order to avoid facing their own souls. One does not become enlightened by imagining figures of light, but by making the darkness conscious."

Well … this, my friends, will be a journey into facing our own souls and illuminating our shadows so we may be set free from the shackles of suffering and embark on a new flight toward rising to the light!

You see, we all have a reason to rise, and it's in rising that we discover our greatness. Perhaps it's your time to rise.

"When the sun rises,
it rises for everyone."
—CUBAN PROVERB

CHAPTER 1

# THE RISING

*"The world is the great gymnasium where
we come to make ourselves strong."*
—SWAMI VIVEKANANDA

The good thing about hitting rock bottom is there is no place lower to fall. You can only rise. That's not rocket science; it's life science. And life science is when you learn through experience, not through mere intellectual understanding.

My rock bottom came like a furious hurricane, cascading into my life and tearing it into itty-bitty pieces. I was a busy working mom and wife, just doing my best. I'd spent thirteen years full-time in the Australian Military, first as aircrew, later commissioned as a nursing officer, and later running my own personal training business and an online mindset coaching business. I was full of the "I can conquer anything" type of mentality and always on the lookout for ways to live my dreams while raising my family. I was doing everything I "should" have been doing (according to society). But society's "shoulds" are kinda ridiculous. Think about it—the world is made up entirely of original individuals, yet there is a silent culture of "one-size-fits-all" for success and happiness. It doesn't make sense. It's downright flawed.

We often get sucked into the all-American dream: find a great job, have a family, take out a mortgage, buy a house, work hard to obtain financial security, take good vacations, and save your pennies for retirement. Fuck! It's exhausting just to read. We really need to upgrade our societal standards.

While we are busy making plans, life is busy screwing them up. That's what happened to me. In one fell swoop, a cascade of events turned my world upside down. In a few short tumultuous years, my dad got dementia and later died; I and my second-born baby nearly died; my husband experienced significant mental health challenges and wanted to end his life; my father-in-law was diagnosed with terminal cancer, and I was juggling my career while still burnt-out from carer's fatigue, grieving the loss of our two babies, among a whole bunch of other stuff. That's the brief version, which I know leaves a lot of unanswered questions. Don't worry, I'll drip feed the details throughout the book, and you'll totally get the reason why rising is the major theme and why rising is the best option when circumstances aren't playing fair. As Viktor Frankl said, "When we are no longer able to change a situation, we are challenged to change ourselves."

Or as I say, when we hit rock bottom, we are forced to rise.

## Rising Is Universal

There is a legendary tale of "rising" all over the world; it's an ancient narrative typically known as the mythical bird, the phoenix, who rises from the ashes in a transformative and fiery rebirth. Although the story of the phoenix varies slightly across cultures, its symbolism is the same all over the world. The phoenix is the symbol of transformation, rebirth, and new beginnings.

Tracing back to even earlier than 500 BC, it was narrated that the phoenix would live for around 500 years. The tale goes that near the end of its life, it would construct a funeral pyre for itself and as it was dying, the phoenix would lie down on the wood and burst into flames, consumed by the fire. Then ... the phoenix would reemerge from the ashes, renewed, more powerful, beautiful, and regal than before. Legend says it would live for another 500 years until the process repeated again.

While this mythical creature was known to the Greeks as "the phoenix," the Egyptians called it the Bennu bird, which literally translates to "rise and shine." The Native Americans called it the Thunderbird; the Chinese use *Fenghuang*; the Japanese have the Hoho bird, and in Jewish culture, the phoenix was called Milcham or Chal and lived in the Garden of Eden. As

# A REASON TO RISE

the story goes, he resisted temptation and was given eternal life by God, therefore becoming an immortal being.

The phoenix represents the universal story that endings are really beginnings and letting go can result in rising stronger. The ultimate transformation for any living thing is a deep and often sacrificial process. The simple caterpillar and tadpole transform themselves through the ultimate metamorphic process into butterfly and frog. To do this, they must sacrifice their old life for a new one.

We humans also morph and transform; we are born into the world and take an epic journey on Earth through lifelong change. Our bodies change; our minds change; our circumstances change, and our transformation is continual until the day we die. And then we take the next transformation.

The cross-cultural theme of renewal and immortality keeps repeating itself through life and legend. I guess in many ways we need these myths and stories to always remind us of the universal principle of change. No one is immune to change. No one is immune to suffering. We all have these in common. But as challenging as life can be, we are also the heroes in our own stories, and rising is part of our story too.

The process of rising isn't easy or even pretty. Much like the phoenix, your wings will get burnt, and you may have wounds and scars—but they won't stop you from flying. As the poetic legend Kahlil Gibran said, "Out of suffering have emerged the strongest souls; the most massive characters are seared with scars."

The process of transformation is more like an initiation into a new world. I know from my own experience, and those of my clients, that it's not all rainbows and lollipops—but I can guarantee you this: Out of the ashes and the dust, you will emerge more beautiful, more divine, and stronger than ever before. You will not be the same person. Nor should you be.

You will be more compassionate. Wiser and kinder. Tougher and softer. You will be clearer and more discerning and yet more loving all at the same time.

As author Haruki Murakami said: "And once the storm is over, you won't remember how you made it through, how you managed to survive. You won't even be sure whether the storm is really over. But one thing is certain. When you come out of the storm, you won't be the same person who walked in. That's what this storm's all about."[1]

Whether you have a broken heart, feel lost in your career path or relationship, or are simply taking an authentic path to self-discovery, ultimately life will dish you out some uncertainty. Life will challenge you and disrupt your plans. Life will test you to your core. Life will make you grieve, laugh, and love. But it will not make you suffer without the opportunity to rise. You can alchemize the pain and transmute the suffering through a strong will to rise and be of service to others.

The great author and philosopher Joseph Campbell said, "Suddenly you're ripped into being alive. And life is pain, and life is suffering, and life is horror, but my god you're alive and it's spectacular."

## Hello, Dark Night of the Soul

I was given my own phoenix rising moments in what felt like a force of nature tearing through my beautiful life. Nothing can really prepare you when an avalanche of life events dismantles your plans and takes your identity with it.

In my twenties, I experienced and overcame stage-one cervical cancer knocking on my door. The journey involved multiple surgeries, and it was one of many life challenges I was forced to RISE from. Really, it was just the beginning.

My first pregnancy was riddled with a condition called hyperemesis gravidarum (HG). HG is a severe condition that causes nonstop vomiting, and nausea is your permanent life state. It's isolating and fatiguing because you can't keep anything down, and, in my case, hospitalization, medication, and IV drips were required to keep me and my baby alive. Luckily for me, the HG eased toward the end of the pregnancy, and our beautiful firstborn son Madden arrived in the world by emergency C-section on 20 October 2015.

In 2018, I fell pregnant again after a deliberate three-and-a-half-year gap. I was prepared for the rough HG journey (as best as one can prepare themselves for continual violent sickness). But nothing could prepare me for the debilitating impact HG served up the second time round.

It took over every area of my life. I couldn't work, parent, connect with loved ones or run my side projects and passions. I felt disconnected and helpless because I was incapacitated. My usual routine, which included being as present as possible in raising Madden, being a wife, daughter, aunt, friend, while maintaining my peak physical performance, health, and fitness, all while juggling a full-time military career plus my mindset coaching business, was now impossible. The only area I excelled in was throwing up, lying down, and feeling terrible. The HG never left. And I mean *never*.

I ended up on a treatment protocol of medication to stop the cyclical vomiting and reflux, sedatives to help me sleep, steroid injections, and regular IV fluids, as I was severely dehydrated. My obstetrician scheduled me in for biweekly hospital admissions just to keep me afloat.

My nursing background meant I left no stone unturned in getting the treatment I needed to survive. I hear of so many HG mamas being dismissed as though it's just morning sickness, or made to feel like they shouldn't take medication, which makes me incredibly sad and frustrated. I had an obstetrician who understood HG, which, combined with my own medical knowledge, using my voice, and advocating my needs and those of my baby, truly made the world of difference in my pregnancy.

Madden missed me and would worry. I was bedridden for months (to the point of pressure sores) and couldn't be the mom I desperately wanted to be. We often played "doctors" as a way to interact when I couldn't leave the bed. That shattered me. My mental health was wavering because I was unable to mother, exercise, and just be me. My husband Dane was taking on all the roles we needed at home and keeping me "in the game" mentally.

On my darkest days, I would often whisper to myself, "Hard isn't impossible" and remember how lucky I was to have a baby human growing inside me. So many women don't get that privilege.

Alongside HG and continual hospitalizations, I had pre-eclampsia (a serious pregnancy condition that involves high blood pressure and protein in the urine and blood) and gestational diabetes (a disorder that occurs in pregnancy and spikes blood sugars, causing diabetes). I had spent my life as a health and fitness professional, and I ended up with diabetes. Seriously? Another identity collapse.

I remember saying to my obstetrician, "I don't think I can do this." Some days were just so hard—it was so hard to believe I had the strength to keep going. Can *I do this?* Regardless of what I thought, I had no choice but to keep pushing through.

With medication and treatment toward the end of the pregnancy, I felt a little more capable and started taking some gentle walks and doing some work. At the time, I was still serving in the military. I began to see a light at the end of the tunnel and a possibility of enjoying the last weeks of my pregnancy.

During this time, some of my old habits crept back in—mainly overdoing things and feeling an obligation at work to do more than I was capable of because I felt guilty for all my time off during my pregnancy—as I tried to gain back a shred of my normal life.

At 31 weeks, yet again destiny intervened. I woke up to a soaking wet bed. *Oh fuck no!* My waters had broken. Panic made its way up my throat. *No! It's too early.*

I rang my midwife and obstetrician, who were practically on speed dial, and we launched into immediate action. Back to hospital I went. Contractions had started.

My obstetrician, also known as a real-life Earth angel, gave me steroid injections so if our baby did come, his lungs would have a fighting chance. I was also loaded with other meds to try and stop the contractions. The idea was to keep bubs safely inside for as long as possible.

I was on strict bed rest. I wasn't to leave the bed except to go to the toilet. Yep, I only had toilet privileges. My obstetrician told me we could be looking at eight to ten weeks, or until bubs decided to make his arrival. I knew that each week inside me would give our baby extra strength and nutrients. Bubs was also in a footling breech position (feet first instead of headfirst)—not the best position to be in for an impending birth.

The situation was intense, and my contractions were still happening despite two medical attempts to pause them. I started to spiral into some old yucky feelings. *Why me? Why am I failing at this? What is the universe wanting from me?* All those old ugly self-deprecating thoughts.

Mmmm ... I had a birth plan, and it was already heading south. My first birth was a C-section, and I was hoping to deliver my second baby vaginally. I decided to start my hypnobirthing practices and meditations to try and gain some peace around the unpredictable situation.

## One Week—Then Showtime

My bed rest lasted just shy of one week before our baby decided it was time. My body was experiencing severe contractions, and bubs was demanding to enter the world. After numerous tests and medical interventions, it became apparent that the baby would be safer outside my body than inside.

What we didn't know at the time was that there was a ticking time bomb inside of me. What we later discovered was that my umbilical cord had formed a tight "true knot." A true knot is a medical complication where the umbilical cord ties a knot and can cut off the blood supply to the baby, among other complications. It is a very rare event that occurs in only 1 percent of pregnancies.[2]

Little did we know that baby and body were very wise and knew that staying inside of me, in fact, decreased the odds of surviving. WOW, my body wasn't failing me at all. She understood the situation and was simply doing what was best.

My body was heading into full-blown labor, and it seemed as though I would finally get the vaginal birth I'd dreamed of. Strangely, I had an overwhelming need to be on all fours with my bum in the air and on both of my elbows in a very specific position (mamas understand the crazy things we do to find an ounce of comfort during the wild throes of labor). So there I was on all fours ready to push this baby out. We were already in the theater, as we were going to prep for another emergency C-section, but baby had other ideas. As it turned out, the position that I intuitively moved into, despite being told to stay on my back as I was being rolled into theater on a trolley, was no accident. What happened next required me to be in that exact position. Thank you, body and divine guidance. Yet again, you just knew.

I said to the midwife, "I'm about to push this baby out." She got me to roll over to conduct a VE (vaginal examination) and see how many centimeters dilated I was. However, instead of checking dilation, they were met with a prolapsed cord. Yes, the umbilical cord had since dropped and extended outside my body. Remember the position I was in? It's the emergency position a mother must adopt in the event of a cord prolapse, and I had moved into it without even knowing this was happening!

Upon the check, there was also a singular foot presenting. The true knot was positioned at the prolapse and my OB immediately knew we weren't dealing with any common emergence or common cord presentation. Not only was the baby in a dangerous footling breech position, but the true knot and prolapse added further complexity—and it didn't end there.

Desperate to get the baby out as soon as possible, not knowing how long the true knot had been present and if adequate oxygen was being supplied, we did what we could to get bubs out vaginally. Though with one foot out, one foot up like a ballerina in my stomach, and a knotted cord that was barely pulsating with life force, it became a compounding medical emergency. Despite best efforts, baby's head got trapped—the medical emergency is known as "head entrapment"—which forced a series of cascading events to unfold.

All I heard was, "Prep for surgery now!" Straight to emergency C-section. It quickly became apparent that the C-section wouldn't go smoothly either. "We're going to have a gray baby," my OB said to the team. I knew what he meant by that, and I felt my whole soul shriek. *Noooooooo!*

I will spare you the gory details ... though let me just say, it was an extremely unconventional theater situation. Rules needed to be broken to save lives. Our incredible obstetrician, who we are so grateful for, also had to take some risks he almost wasn't prepared to take. It was an extremely primitive and almost barbaric medical situation, and the stakes were high—no, they were catastrophic. Protocols just about went out the window. Theater preparation checks were nonexistent. There was no time for proper anesthesia protocols, no time for taking records or checking equipment. In fact, I remember that my OB had donned just one blue glove (no sterile gloves in other words) and my midwife literally squirted some Betadine in the general direction of my abdomen. I have a very vivid memory of a wardsman holding up a hospital blanket as a makeshift drape. It was a chaotic and traumatic scene that affected everyone, as you can imagine: the medical team, the nonmedical team involved, my husband Dane, my obstetric team, of course me—heck, anyone who heard our story and understood the situation.

Let me just say, it didn't end there. The chaos dial kept dialing, and I was about to experience a pain I will never ever be able to describe.

My spinal anesthetic failed to take. Just let that sentence set in for a moment. A spinal anesthetic (or spinal) involves intricately injecting local anesthetics and other medication into the subarachnoid space to completely numb the nerves and give a full anesthetic response and pain relief during a C-section. My spinal had failed, and amid all the chaos, my C-section had commenced. I felt every bit of the initial cut and opening during the surgery. *Fucking ouch!* Yes, I was cut open while awake, without anesthesia taking effect. I truly cannot describe the pain, and I don't think I will ever be able to, for there isn't a word that can even come close to communicating what I experienced.

Due to the medical emergency and positioning of baby, my C-section also had to be both transverse and vertical (so imagine not just a single cut across the bikini line, but also one up vertically through my abdomen). I screamed and lifted off the table like I was undergoing an exorcism. "Stop! I can Feel it!" Honestly, I left my body from the indescribable pain as shock set in. I remember seeing blood spurt across my vision to a wall behind me, and then I saw *nothing*. The anesthetist knocked me out as quickly as possible. The time between feeling *everything* to feeling nothing felt like forever, and I had so much adrenaline racing through my body.

The out-of-body experience ended up creating a deeper connection to Source. It was a life-transitioning moment, and I really didn't know if I would live or, worse, if my baby would live. In that moment, I wondered if I was heading to heaven. I felt like I was between worlds, and the connection to Spirit was strong. Somewhere, halfway between birth, death, and heaven, my soul surrendered. I relinquished my own human power and allowed something wiser, stronger, and grander to control my destiny and that of my unborn baby. I was about to experience a rebirth. Although my body was still in hell.

Poor Dane was witnessing it all unfold and, due to the chaos in the theater, without any support. The staff had no time to worry about him, as seconds really mattered. He didn't know if I had died on the table. He also didn't know if his baby was alive. His protective instincts and family-oriented leadership had nowhere to go. He looked on helplessly, mute and in shock, observing a nightmare scene involving his wife and baby and praying for a miracle.

Somehow, among the medical exorcism, confusion, shock, blood, and chaos, the medical team miraculously brought our son into the world. He was not responding. The pediatrician attempted to revive him as Dane watched on, his eyes apparently darting between me and his newborn son. He didn't know who was alive or dead. The pediatrician and emergency team kept working on our baby. They weren't giving up. His time without oxygen was unknown.

Fast-forward to what felt like a lifetime for Dane, and finally, on the ninth day of the seventh month on the ninth hour at the seventh minute 2019 (how is that for a sign?), our son Beckham took his first breath. Miraculously, his premature and exhausted little lungs and body were brought back to life. He was on oxygen and needing special care—but he was alive. And so was I. *Just.*

Let's also remember that we were two months premature at this point. So following the harrowing events of the birth, we started our journey as a preemie family, doing our best with a premature newborn, leaving him in the care of the hospital and Earth angel midwives and doctors for the fight of his life.

Meanwhile, my body wore the fresh scars of the traumatic scene. I was immediately put on an intense regime of intravenous antibiotics, as, given the situation, my risk of infection and potentially sepsis or return surgery for clean out was high.

It was like a movie scene—Dane, our **OB-GYN**, and the medical team all looked stunned. Every one of us felt the experience deeply. In many instances, the decisions my obstetrician made were lifesaving and risky, yet he did what he needed to do. He went beyond what I believe very few would be willing to do to save my life and that of our baby. To me, he is an Earth angel, a warrior of life, and I would never want anyone else in this world to have been there to manage the harrowing situation that involved multiple medical emergencies at once.

The aftermath was a cascade of emotions and events—gratefulness for surviving, bewilderment at the unusual rarity of the situation, shock, prayer, joy, pain, painkillers, and a premature baby doing his best to thrive.

My spiritual experience through all the hell had transformed the way I saw life, and I was ready to live my highest ideals. I was so glad that God didn't give me the vaginal birth I'd hoped for—the pressure from the exit would have put pressure on the true knot, and, without a doubt, I would have delivered a stillborn. If I had gone even one day longer into my pregnancy, the result could have been catastrophic. I was a ticking time bomb. My baby's life was safer outside, and my body and divine guidance just knew! I felt surrendered—life knew what it was doing. There was an innate wisdom that made my body go into labor early, made our little man demand to come into the world prematurely.

Seeing his tiny little body alive and watching his little chest move up and down with his breath took my breath away. Our little miracle.

## The Calm and the Storm

Beckham started to show all the good signs of a thriving baby: mainly breastfeeding and growing. Dane and I spent countless hours with the medical team, going through the events and debriefing. We were all affected, and the hospital and team were of course big about debriefing and making sure everyone was managing OK after the ordeal. All those debriefs and meetings while confronting were also cathartic. We had shared a sliding doors moment with that team; our lives were literally in their hands. And yes, it could have gone down a different path, a terrible one that involved a lot of loss, heartache, grief, and pain.

During one of our meetings, the psychological staff mentioned a common theme that can occur after a traumatic experience. They said, "After about six months, feelings can emerge." They told us about PTSD (post-traumatic stress disorder) and how it can develop and show up.

At the time, we heard the words but were in such a good place that we reassured them we were doing well. I was enjoying my second lease on life. Food tasted like heaven (remember my HG prevented me from keeping anything down for seven months), and, well, we were alive. Life was good, given the alternative. Our usual life had been turned upside down, and we would never be the same people again.

The day of Beckham's birth, Dane resigned from his job. He was project managing in the building industry, and his phone was going crazy. No one seemed to respect what had just happened, and it was taking its toll on him. I had been down that road myself, and I recognized the burnout and saw the lack of care and support he had around him and the pressures of his job. "Just quit!" I said between pumping breast milk and getting my IV antibiotic medication through the drip. We both knew that nothing mattered more than our family. So quit, he did. He wrote the resignation letter in the hospital that night, and we sent it. Life never felt so goddamn empowering, even though I was still in a wheelchair with my belly all cut to shreds. "We'll work it out," I reassured him. I knew we would.

Fast-forward, and only a prem-family knows the immense and monumental celebration of the day you get to take your baby home! That moment, I'll always remember.

When we finally arrived home and our boys were united, we were a whole family. I had never felt so lucky. Sure, we had our challenges—intense physio for me, oral antibiotics I would need to continue for quite some time, a preemie baby and his needs, and of course our firstborn toddler—but at least our family was complete.

Right on cue, just like the psychologist had warned, six months after our birth trauma experience, Dane started struggling with his mental health. He coped in silence and fought the strange thoughts and emotions that were tormenting him. Night sweats and nightmares began to interrupt his sleep, and he became increasingly exhausted and unable to cope with these foreign feelings.

I was on full throttle, trying to make up for lost time, juggle the kids' needs, and head back to work to keep us financially afloat. Dane and I were like a tag team, doing what we could to survive. On top of everything, my dad, who was suffering from early onset dementia, was suddenly in rapid decline, and Mom was struggling as his primary caregiver after a decade. She was starting to burn out and needed some respite. I was trying to help from afar but felt useless, so I began traveling back and forth between home and my parents' house to help Mom take care of Dad. Dane was still struggling mentally, and now I was in and out of our home, desperately trying to keep Dad, Dane, my young family, and myself together.

Our life started to swirl into a tsunami of unusual and challenging events. In this same tumultuous period, Dane's dad, Terry, was diagnosed with terminal myeloma and told he only had six months to live. Going back and forth between helping Mom and being there for Dane and my in-laws, with the kids in tow, it was all a blur of survival, with everyone just holding on for dear life.

I worried that Terry's diagnosis would tip Dane over the edge. When I was away helping mom take care of Dad, I was tormented by terrible visions of finding Dane succumbed to his suicidal ideations when I returned. Dane was severely unwell and having suicidal thoughts. Dad's dementia was progressing to a dangerous stage, his life hanging by a thread. Mom was burnt out and suffering immense carer's fatigue. Terry was fighting for his life. And I felt torn. My mind was constantly telling me, *I need to help Dane, I need to help Dad, I need to help Mom, I need to be there for my in-laws, I need to take care of Madden and Beckham, I need to find a way through.*

My brain couldn't fathom what was happening, and I was running to keep up, praying that we'd be OK. I felt helpless against all these big problems pounding down on us all at once. I felt as if Dane, Terry, and Dad were all heading toward a horrific destiny that I couldn't stop. But I would sure as hell try.

I wondered if this was the dark night of the soul that mystics refer to. The place where you feel lost and abandoned and desperate. I wondered what the hell the universe was doing to us. Why was all this crazy terrible shit happening? I really didn't know.

For the first time in my life, I consciously surrendered (this time without anesthetic and a near-death experience). I communed with something greater than me and asked for strength. I didn't know our way out. I didn't know why we were experiencing such life-threatening moments one after another. I didn't know the grand plan of our destiny. I needed to step back and trust something greater than me that did know. I thought about the wisdom of the universe when Beckham was born. How it knew something that I did not. How it conspired for me, not against me. I had to take a wild leap of faith and trust that somehow, among the shitstorm of painful events, some greater story was behind the next chapter we were about to enter.

I was in the dark night of the soul, but I was not without faith. Sure, it was shaky, but it was still there like a little light shining down a long black tunnel. Although I couldn't control all the moving pieces and the unfolding destinies of the people I loved, I could control the part that I played. I could give up and feel helpless, or I could RISE and use the powers that had been gifted to me—my thoughts, my beliefs, my skills, my knowledge—to co-conspire and cocreate along the way.

I knew the choice was mine. I could rise without guaranteed outcomes, or I could watch from the sideline and hope for the best, also without guaranteed outcomes. I decided to RISE.

I didn't know how that would look or if it would matter, but I knew that after the most painful contractions in life, there is a new birth. After the dark, there is a dawn.

I clung to trust and hope. I clung to them like a life raft, praying it would take us to safety. In the meantime, I knew I would paddle like hell and do all I could to navigate the small parts of this grand plan that I could control. It was risky—but what other choices were there?

Author Caroline Myss said, "The dark night of the soul

is a journey into light, a journey from your darkness into the strength and hidden resources of your soul." I somehow sensed that this journey, no matter how harrowing, was going to be just that—a journey into the hidden resources of my soul. A deep voyage into unknown and untapped places within. A pilgrimage into the palace of my soul.

I did not know if my choice to rise would make any difference to the outcomes, but I figured trying was better than expecting more miracles to beam down and bless me. I would pray for miracles and try to be one at the same time.

And that's the adventure I entered.

CHAPTER 2

# THE MOST POWERFUL DECISION OF YOUR LIFE

Deciding you want more from your life is a powerful decision. Deciding to RISE is a life-altering one.

When you arrive at this junction, you don't just change yourself; you change the world around you. The decisions you make impact your life and the lives of others. It's a wild and mind-blowing responsibility!

Wanting more out of life and deciding to RISE to get what you want doesn't mean you're not grateful for what you already have. It doesn't mean you're not satisfied or fulfilled either.

It means that you feel there's more inside of you to become, give, and contribute. It means there's more of your potential to unleash! It means there's more you want to express and more dreams to create. If you're still breathing and still searching for your life's purpose and grand potential, it means you're not done yet. There's more waiting for you. There's more you want to give.

**Rising can also be a radical way to stop settling for mediocre. Making the decision to rise is part of embracing your desire for more.**

If you've ever been to a Tony Robbins seminar, you'll know that one of the first things he does is get the entire audience to raise their standards. He basically makes it his 101 class and hollers, "Raise your standards!"

You see, the moment you accept and embrace that deep yearning inside is the moment you stop fighting the frustration, the complacency, and the procrastination. You face the demon that says, "Wanting more is selfish!"

You stand up and say, "I'm not done yet. There's more for me. There's more from me."

Wanting more is not selfish if what you desire serves other people, or your family, or yourself. Rising isn't egotistical; it's powerful. It's your way of raising yourself to a new level.

Wanting more can, of course, be a trap to some. Constantly craving more things like money, attention, awards, a bigger house, better spouse, or shinier car can feel like trying to fill up a bucket with a hole in it. You can keep filling it up with more, more, more, but it will continue to leak, leaving you empty.

But there is a way you can rise above craving and rise to your dreams without compromising your integrity and values. Let me explain.

## Rising the Right Way

Many psychologists believe that we have a base "set point" and after experiencing big highs or lows in life, we often return to our common emotional baseline. The fancy term they give this is "hedonic adaptation" or being on the "hedonic treadmill."

For example, you win a major award or land a new promotion and after that major exciting win, over time the thrill wears off, and you return to your normal baseline. So you then look for the next thing that will give you the next high or achievement.

On the flip side, you experience a major loss—perhaps you lose a loved one or your beloved pet, and you feel grief-stricken. At first, you think you will never be able to cope, as the grief is overbearing. Although you mourn and mourn, eventually you find yourself experiencing pockets of time where you feel OK, where you accidentally smile and feel a morsel of joy. Over time, you are changed—and so is life—but eventually you return to your common baseline. You're a little different, yes, but nevertheless OK.

This adaptation we all experience can be quite baffling.

Humans are skilled at adaptation; it's how we survive and continue to survive. But in our great ability to adapt, we have also adapted to seeking more and more and more. We have set ourselves up to crave more and never quite feel satisfied.

Now, as I said earlier, desiring more isn't the problem. In fact, I encourage it. The problem is when we fall onto the hamster wheel of craving more and more and end up chasing the cycle of bigger attainment rather than looking at what is personally meaningful to us, what sparks our inner joy, what makes life worth living.

**When we align our authentic self with our goals and dreams, the craving cycle isn't a relentless hamster wheel; it becomes an extraordinary hero's journey of self-development, contribution, service, and pride.**

Although success often naturally follows, it isn't because you are craving things just for a next serotonin or dopamine hit, or to brag on social media. It's because living your best and most authentic life is more thrilling than any drug, any medal, or any false ideal. It's what you've been seeking your entire life.

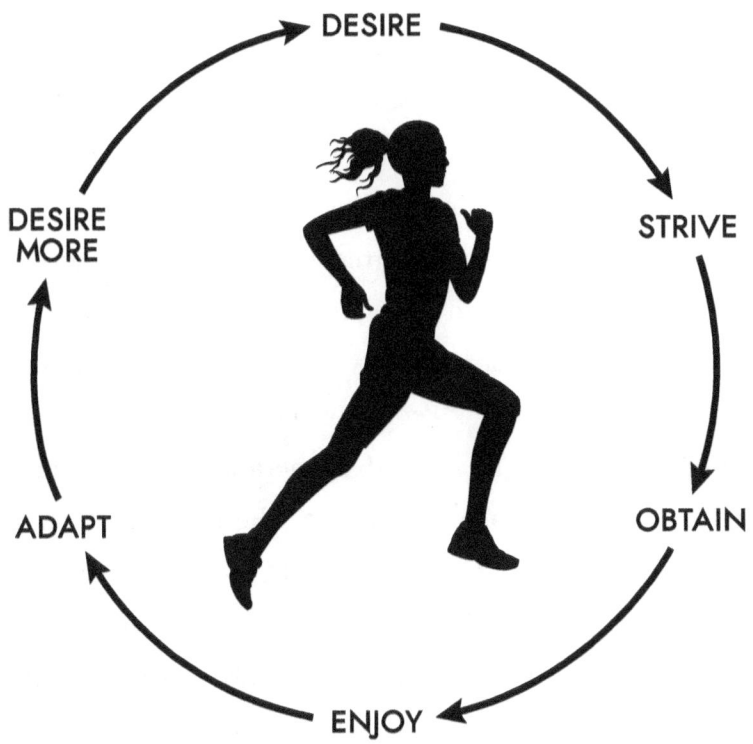

So if you find yourself chasing or craving the next shiny object or next experience over and over again, the good news is, you can actually change this relationship. Investing in long-term habits, such as expressing gratitude, consciously creating a better you, engaging in selfless service or regular acts of kindness, mindfulness practices, investing in important relationships, and engaging in a meaningful long-term vision for yourself and your life, can all reduce "hedonic adaptation."

So, in a nutshell, craving more is *not* the problem—not balancing this craving with an enduring meaningful life that accentuates your purpose, perspective, personality, and passion, however, is.

Although I am an advocate of "raise your standards," I believe we must do so in *alignment* with our values, our purpose, and our passion. Not just because we want "more stuff." Abundance is certainly a part of it; it's just not everything.

Ancients have been making great decisions about "more" for a long time. The desire to do good things for the next generation is a prime motivation of many ancient cultures. The Native American *Haudenosaunee* ("People of the Longhouse") Iroquois philosophy is called the Seventh Generation Principle and is based on their cultural wisdom that "the decisions we make today should result in a sustainable world seven generations into the future."[1]

Indigenous Australians spent thousands of years living in harmony with the land, the elements, and each other. Their songlines, stories, ceremonies, cultural practices, knowledge, and wisdom all get passed from generation to generation.

Making decisions is something we cannot avoid—our ancestors couldn't avoid it either—so we might as well make our decisions matter! We might as well make incredibly powerful decisions that create the change we want to see.

Even in today's modern society, experts suggest we make around 35,000 decisions each day, some tiny—like what to eat or wear—and others that carry more responsibility—like whether to apply for a new position at work, enroll in a new course, or spend some money on a holiday.[2] A lot of the daily grind is about decisions, and we are always trying to "see ahead" and calculate the potential risk or consequences of each one.

- If I eat the chocolate brownie, then I will have broken my health streak.
- If I don't enroll the kids in swimming lessons, they may not be equipped with enough skill.
- If I cook the tuna casserole, Billy won't like it, but Madeline will.
- If I say "yes" to a coffee with my friend, I won't have time to finish my essay.
- If I change banks, I need to redo all the paperwork. Should I wait until next month?
- If my daughter needs braces, will I need to cancel our Netflix subscription for a little while?
- Should I invite Aunty Mary to the party? She got blind drunk last time and tried to kiss the neighbor.

We are doomed to make decisions. We are a product of all the little and big choices we make. And here's the kicker—as your level of responsibility increases, so does the number of choices you have to make. As American author John C. Maxwell famously said, "Life is a matter of choices, and every choice you make makes you."

This is why CEOs are such powerful decision-makers. They make so many decisions each day that they become really good at doing just that. McKinsey research suggests that many executives spend nearly 40 percent of their work time making decisions.[3] If that's the percentage for executives, imagine the percentage for moms, or moms who are both executives and mothers. Omg! The stats don't exist because, let's be honest, it would potentially mind-bend the researchers.

## Beware—Decision Fatigue

Making decisions can be exhausting. I know a mom of three who once said to me, "The decision of what to cook for dinner every night is tiring me out." Her eldest was 17 years old, so you can imagine how hard it had become to be creative in the kitchen after all those years.

People struggle with small decisions (like what to cook for dinner) and big decisions (like whether to divorce or make a career change) so much that they actually get something called "decision fatigue."[4] Sound familiar?

Basically, decision fatigue is feeling exhausted or depleted in your capacity to make decisions. Research suggests that individuals who experience decision fatigue often start to exhibit symptoms such as:

- Avoidant behaviors (like putting off key decisions).
- Taking a passive approach to key decisions, or heavily procrastinating.
- Making impulsive or irrational decisions (just to get it over with).
- Higher levels of disengagement in decision-making activities.
- Lethargy and/or general tiredness.[5]

When I was a nurse, I could really relate to decision fatigue, not necessarily when I was at work but rather when I got home. As a nurse, you make decisions all day, every day, and the stakes are high—people's lives depend on your decisions and observations. You can't afford to make a wrong decision! No one wants a nurse, let alone a surgeon, with decision fatigue, right?

But because I was making big decisions every day, when I got home, I didn't really feel like making those small decisions, like what to eat or whether I should change my insurance policies. To be quite frank, I didn't give a fuck some days. I mean, the patient in my emergency department who needed lifesaving care got my attention, but whether to have chicken or beef on my plate really didn't matter.

I soon began to think about decisions that required my energy and those that didn't matter too much. I became selective about my decisions. And this, my friends, was a game changer!

During extreme crises, the decisions I needed to make became clearer! Sometimes I made them well—like getting Dad the best care possible and advocating for his welfare. Other times, I missed the mark. I avoided my husband's urgent mental health issues because I thought there were "more urgent" things happening, and I didn't realize how rapidly his health was declining. I wasn't conscious of the gravity of the situation, as I was overwhelmed from being pushed and pulled in different directions. My decision fatigue clouded my awareness.

The interesting thing about being in a prolonged crisis is that your "normal" becomes blurred because you're in a state of chronic stress and fatigue. For some people, that state of abnormal chronic stress results in a breakdown. For others, it can be the catalyst for a breakthrough.

One of the biggest, hardest, best decisions I ever made was deciding I wanted more for my life. I wanted more freedom, more joy, more connection, more money, more good things happening, and less shit to handle.

I had to breakthrough or breakdown and, well … I wasn't sure which way it would go. But the decision to raise my standards and amplify my passion and purpose was one that changed the course of my life. Deciding to RISE above my circumstances and create a better life for myself and my family radically moved the needle and shifted my baseline.

- I raised the bar BIG TIME for some of my BIG decisions.
- And I lowered the bar for some of my smaller decisions.

You see, I couldn't afford to play small anymore. Something big had to change in my life because I couldn't deal with the current conditions of my reality. I wasn't living my full potential. I simply wasn't. I was merely surviving a shitstorm! I was white-knuckling my way through life, just trying to keep everything from falling further apart. What I didn't know was that making powerful decisions would steer me toward the desired outcomes and directing energy at making the right decisions would, in fact, alter my very existence.

## Reasons to RISE (or Not!)

The moment I began to take charge of my decisions was the day I took charge of my life. I decided that some things simply were no longer acceptable in my life. I needed to scale up. I needed to fire up, and I needed to RISE like a phoenix from the rubble of fuckery.

The reasons why we don't rise are many. In fact, there are many more "reasons" to NOT rise at times. Reasons like:

- It's too scary.
- What will other people think of me?
- What if I fail?
- What if I embarrass myself?
- I'm not good enough to succeed.
- I'm not worthy enough.
- I'm not strong enough.
- I'm not smart enough.
- I'm not powerful enough.
- I'm not ready.
- I'm not capable.
- I'm not able to because (fill in the blank).
- It could change my relationship.
- It could change my life.
- It could disrupt my plans.
- I don't have the time.
- I don't have the money.
- I don't have the energy.

- I don't have the willpower.
- I don't have the ability.
- I don't have the motivation.

The list of ~~reasons~~ excuses goes on.

What I noticed was that once the pain of just surviving became so great, my desire for change became a need and a must! Staying the same was becoming too painful, and *not* changing was a scary thought.

It's often in those moments that you think quietly, *Is this it? Is this all there fucking is to show for my hard work and effort?*

It's a confronting realization. Sometimes downright demoralizing.

But as the great author and lecturer Joseph Campbell said, "You must give up the life you planned in order to have the life that is waiting for you." He believed that is what the hero's journey is all about.

Life calls you to a great adventure. Your unique adventure that only you know. It's up to you if you answer the call. It doesn't guarantee an easy path, but it does guarantee the path of fulfilling your greatest destiny.

Fulfilling your greatest destiny is a reason to RISE.

If you look at the reasons *not* to RISE, they are all about fear. Scared of failure, scared of what other people might think, scared of uncertainty, scared of risk.

If you look at the reasons to RISE, they are all about growth, potential, and passion.

**Reasons to Rise**
- To fulfill your greatest destiny.
- To see what you can achieve.
- To transform your current state of mind.
- To transform your current circumstances.
- To answer the call to adventure.
- To fulfill your potential.
- To grow.
- To defy the odds.
- To finally do what the fuck you *really* want to do!
- To not die wondering what could have been or should have been.

## You Are the CEO of Your Life

Decisions can become your most powerful superpower. They aren't always easy, and they need to be congruent with you.

The key to decisions is making them in alignment with who you are and the values you hold. Are you making decisions to uphold a certain social mask or because you feel obligated to someone? Or are you making decisions that feed your heart and soul?

For example, one of my clients, Rosa, was avoiding making a decision to leave her retail job. She had been in the same role for over twenty-six years but was tired and bored. She didn't want to let her boss down, as she knew how hard it was for her to find reliable staff. She had become good friends with her boss and really cared for her and her family. Rosa was the most reliable and diligent employee and kept putting off her dream plan because she couldn't let her boss down. She really wanted to go on a long road trip around Australia with her husband and then work casual at her daughter's florist shop. Rosa's superpowers (compassion, reliability, and diligence) had become the bondage that kept her tied to her job.

When I asked Rosa why she was choosing to stay unhappy instead of choosing her joy, she said, "Because I feel so terrible letting my boss down. She has been so good to me over the years!"

When I suggested to Rosa that she had been equally good to her boss, she dismissed it, saying, "I'm just doing my job!"

I challenged her. I suggested she was actually doing way MORE than her job. Her job was to turn up, run the staff, be nice to customers, tally the money, and record the daily sales. It wasn't her job to put her life on hold and stay in her mundane role for the rest of her days to please someone else.

Rosa was avoiding making decisions that allowed her to get what she wanted. She was blocking her joy, her destiny, and her highest life due to obligation and guilt.

Rosa isn't alone. Many of us block our own happiness and dreams because we don't feel deserving of them. We may think, *Who am I to have great success, or great happiness? I'm just average. Crazy dreams are just for celebrities and influencers and rockstars.*

I call bullshit!

Your dreams are like your fingerprints—unique to you! No

one else has the exact same ones, and it's up to you to fulfill your own dreams. No one is going to do it for you.

You are the captain of your ship, the CEO of your life. You call the shots. You decide what you will and won't settle for.

If you've been settling for a life of struggle and desperation, you can decide to create a life where you thrive and feel passionately alive. It may not change in an instant, but it takes an instant to decide.

When you decide you will no longer settle for pain and struggle as your 24-7 job but will instead instill some new beliefs about what is possible for you, change becomes the result.

## The Most Powerful Decisions of Your Life

Wanting *more* is not dirty or shameful. Wanting more love and healing and less pain and grief is human. Wanting more abundance and less scarcity is totally A-OK. This world is abundant by nature, right? So you only want what is naturally here.

I give you a full-blown permission slip to want more in and from your life. Without making the decision to want more, I wouldn't have all the blessings I have now.

Why not make the most powerful decision of your life right now? Why not decide what you will no longer settle for? Go ahead ... make that list. It could be that you'll no longer settle for a shitty relationship, a half-done manuscript, a habit of self-neglect, a mediocre mindset, financial debt, a crappy job.

*What I will no longer settle for ...*

..................................................................................................

..................................................................................................

..................................................................................................

..................................................................................................

..................................................................................................

..................................................................................................

..................................................................................................

..................................................................................................

..................................................................................................

..................................................................................................

Now, if you're gonna ditch some old aspects of your life, you might as well be intentional about what you'd like to invite into your life. Make powerful decisions about where you are going, who you're hanging out with, and what you want. As Brené Brown says in *Rising Strong,* "People who wade into discomfort and vulnerability and tell the truth about their stories are the real badasses." These decisions matter! They make up your life.

So, let's get to work ... It's time to be a real badass about your life and your future life.

*What experiences do I want to invite and attract into my life?*

*Which people do I wish to stay connected to?*

..............................................................................................................................

..............................................................................................................................

..............................................................................................................................

..............................................................................................................................

..............................................................................................................................

..............................................................................................................................

..............................................................................................................................

*What type of people do I want to invite and attract into my life?*

..............................................................................................................................

..............................................................................................................................

..............................................................................................................................

..............................................................................................................................

..............................................................................................................................

..............................................................................................................................

..............................................................................................................................

..............................................................................................................................

*Where do I want to be in two years' time? Write it out in detail.*

*Where do I want to be in five or ten years?*

*If I see myself RISING, what does it look like? Who am I when I do this? What mental traits do I exhibit?*

......................................................................................................................................

......................................................................................................................................

......................................................................................................................................

......................................................................................................................................

......................................................................................................................................

......................................................................................................................................

......................................................................................................................................

......................................................................................................................................

......................................................................................................................................

......................................................................................................................................

......................................................................................................................................

......................................................................................................................................

......................................................................................................................................

......................................................................................................................................

......................................................................................................................................

......................................................................................................................................

Scan the QR code to check out the powerful collection of *A Reason to Rise* bonus tools and resources, collated as my gift to you for choosing to RISE.

## Decisions We Don't Make— Intergenerational Trauma

Although we are in charge of our decisions, there are many decisions that were made generations before us that affect us today. Many studies have shown that what happened in one generation can affect the next, and the next. This can happen in both positive and negative ways.

The most known impact of this is intergenerational trauma. Intergenerational trauma has been studied significantly in recent times, and research has highlighted the fact that what happens during our grandparents' lifetime, or the lifetimes of previous generations, can affect us today, even without having experienced the same traumatic events.[6] It acts like an invisible chain of trauma that is stored in our genes, bodies, and psyches. Intergenerational trauma has been studied for such groups as Holocaust survivors, prisoners of war, Aboriginal communities and the Stolen Generation, refugees, indigenous populations of Canada and the Americas, and other minority groups.[7]

Bessel van der Kolk, author of the bestselling book *The Body Keeps the Score*, describes trauma as not merely an event in the past but also something that leaves a firm imprint in our psyche and body. The reason I bring this up is because understanding this complex cycle helped me understand my dad, my grandfather, and therefore myself.

My mom's heritage is a unique combination of Filipino Spaniards. My dad's side is Scottish and Irish. My grandfather (my dad's dad) was a decorated war hero and ended up as a prisoner of war (POW) during World War II. My grandmother (my dad's mom) was also a war veteran, and they both were involved in WWII. This meant that my dad was raised by his aunt rather than his parents, as they were away in the war for much of his childhood.

My grandfather survived a Japanese POW camp, where the prisoners were tortured and starved. When he returned from the war, he came home with silent but obvious demons. My dad was the youngest child and often the target of his dad's uncontrollable temper.

My dad was born during the time of polio, which he contracted, resulting in him having a deformed leg and foot that was much shorter than the other. He walked with a prominent limp, which embarrassed his father, and he was often ridiculed.

Due to his condition, he wasn't able to be a frontline soldier. He was always embarrassed about his limp, and, whenever anyone asked what had happened, he told them he had been in a motorbike accident. He kept this lie his entire life, almost as he believed it himself.

My grandfather was a troubled man when he returned from war. He became increasingly violent and abusive, especially to my dad. He seemed to channel all his hate toward my father and often bashed him to a pulp. My dad hated him. A decorated war hero to the world, but a violent tyrant behind closed doors.

After the war, my grandfather spent the majority of his time in a military rehab facility and was constantly on medication to "manage" his violent temper and outbursts. The military would send him home for several days for "family integration." However, it was more like a family humiliation than integration for my dad. My grandfather was mentally tormented, and the military rehab personnel had to visit the house on several occasions and physically restrain him (even using massive force like punches and grappling him to the floor) to inject him with a sedative. He was out of control, and my dad was the merciless victim of his hatred.

My grandfather's inner warfare became intolerable for him. One day, while at home, he took matters into his own hands. At the time, my dad was a young teenager. He had been playing outside before entering the house to see his father walk slowly down the stairs with a military sword in his hand. I don't know if my grandfather expected to come face-to-face with his son at that moment. Perhaps he thought it was destined to be witnessed by him—I don't know. Either way, it didn't stop him from what he was about to do.

My grandfather stood in a strong stance in front of my dad, his youngest son, drew his military sword, and let out a piercing warrior-like scream as he thrust the blade deep into his own stomach, circling the sword around and around to disembowel himself, and ultimately end his life.

My dad stood there witnessing the act of what the Japanese samurai warriors refer to as *seppuku*, but we know it in the West as *hara-kiri*. His father died by suicide in the backyard of our family home. My dad stood watching, his freeze response perhaps rooting him to witness the tragic end of his father.

The paradoxical thing about my grandfather's suicide was that he chose to end his life in the way that is traditionally rooted in Japanese culture—the same culture that held him as a prisoner of war. Although *seppuku* declined in the late nineteenth century along with the samurai, some military personnel from World War II still practiced it. Some saw it as a way to die a "noble death" and control their destiny rather than surrender. The history of *seppuku* is long and entrenched in both cultural and ritualistic practices that are ancient and difficult for Western minds to understand. In ancient Japanese culture, *seppuku* can be noble, or it can be obligatory (a forced self-execution for unfavorable acts). Either way, it was the way my grandfather decided to end his life.

According to some historians, some ancient Asian cultures believed that the soul rests in the belly and slitting the gut open sets the spirit free. The samurai believed that only true samurai could perform the act, as one had to be mentally brave and strong to do it. Part of their ritual included not grimacing, hesitating, or showing an expression of fear or shock.

I am not saying my grandfather's suicide was a noble act; it was torturous and the act of a very ill man. However, understanding the way he viewed his self-execution allowed us to deal with his act and understand the implications of intergenerational trauma. Understanding what my dad endured and witnessed allowed me to gain more understanding about his unresolved trauma and how it played out through our family.

The interesting thing about all of this is during my own deep healing and spiritual work, I witnessed this all unfolding in my mind's eye as if I were viewing it for real. It was a visual and visceral experience. My entire being responded. It was as if it was also stored in my brain and body, and the healing was cathartic yet incredibly harrowing to release.

At the time, I didn't understand the impact and secondary implications of generational trauma. Psychology and science are now revealing what we intuitively recognize: we are indeed affected by others' experiences.

I can also see how the pattern of self-reliance became so ingrained in my family. My dad was self-reliant—he had to be. His parents were posted overseas during the war, and he had to take care of himself from an early age. His aunty was a great support, but he developed a lot of independence and self-reliance earlier than most.

A culture of self-reliance was also established within our family. My mom and dad raised us toward personal self-reliance, and while I was raised in a loving household, my brother and I often fended for ourselves. We stayed home by ourselves from an early age, taking care of ourselves and the day-to-day duties. We took ourselves to school and were expected to be radically responsible and accountable at a young age. It was the way we were raised. No mollycoddling.

Despite hating his own dad's behavior, my dad followed generational patterns of alcohol-fueled domestic violence and abuse. He had violent bouts and would become a man we didn't recognize. My mom and dad were each other's everything, yet when Dad would fly off into fits of unresolved anger and rage, Mom was often his target. It was mind-bending for me and my brother as kids. Our beloved dad, who loved his family so much, his family that he would do anything for, could also turn into someone totally different. We always stood up for Mom, yet we could see Dad's struggles and knew that, underneath his random outbursts, he was a hurt man repeating the pattern of hurting others.

Luckily for me, my family dealt with this head-on over decades, especially as us kids developed as teens and beyond. We started boldly standing up for what we knew to be right, often stood in the way of arguments, and supported Dad with his alcohol issue. To the credit of both Dad and our family unit, and after six decades of heavy drinking, he became sober in his 70s, when the alcohol-fueled violence peaked and the cycle finally ended. Although the damage caused had been immense, we were finally able to close this chapter of our lives.

In the last stages of my dad's life, as his body and mind shut down, I saw his heart and soul completely transform and heal from a life of anger and violence. Although he was a man who showed so much loyalty, love, and dedication to his family, he was also a man who couldn't fully show affection and could barely say "I love you" when we were growing up. However, the man he was in his latter years and on his deathbed was completely different—transformed.

Through our own modeling of love and change, compassion, forgiveness, and understanding, along with undeniable support,

I saw the cycle of intergenerational trauma collapse inside my dad before he died. He finally forgave himself for his misgivings; he dropped the final walls of his former anguish and became pure LOVE. He loved Mom and his children with all his heart, and he healed a lot of the pain he had suffered, in turn, healing a version of me I didn't even know existed.

Interestingly, our family home remained a very decorated military home, with medals and photos and memorabilia spanning the walls. Even the sword my grandfather used to end his life was still there. I believe the sense of nostalgia and our proud military history somehow helped Dad. It's a strange cycle … but the trauma that hurt also became part of the healing balm of which Dad was proud.

## Healing Intergenerational Trauma

Healing intergenerational trauma is both mysterious and possible. Researchers, geneticists, and psychologists are all looking at the myriad of ways trauma runs through our lineages and impacts us.[8]

However, we must also look at the fact that if we have intergenerational trauma, then perhaps we also have intergenerational wisdom and resilience that we can "pass on" to others. Why should it all be negative? In fact, psychiatry researchers have explored how communicating in an open and loving way between generations helps foster resilience, connection, and healing. When survivors of trauma share their stories with their children or grandchildren, the survivors are able to deal with the past better, and new lines of bonding communication open up between them.[9]

I believe that trauma keeps playing out when we stay silent and don't address it. Silence about the past and the pain only exacerbates the issue, spilling out as anger, addiction, abuse, substance abuse, and suicide. Alternatively, sharing stories allows us to be seen, heard, and cared for.

Author of *It Didn't Start with You*, Mark Wolynn, an expert on generational trauma, says, "Remaining silent about family pain is rarely an effective strategy for healing it. The suffering will surface again at a later time, often expressing in the fears or symptoms of a later generation."[10] He explains, "Just as we inherit our eye color and blood type, we also inherit the residue from traumatic events that have taken place in our family. Illness, depression, anxiety, unhappy relationships and financial challenges can all be forms of this unconscious inheritance."[11]

Intergenerational trauma can gain additional momentum in families who try to "cover up the past," keep the trauma secret, or manipulate the truth. This can then lead to setting up unstable coping mechanisms, avoidant behavior, or repressive tendencies. Hence, the prevalence of "family secrets" can often be a maladaptive way to save face or maintain a good name. This happens in all cultures for many different reasons all over the world.

In many cultures, particularly in some Asian and Middle Eastern cultures, "keeping face" to other families or societal standards requires a lot of masking, not telling the truth, and complying to certain protocols and expectations. In the West, we also see this play out in more nuanced ways, for example, keeping domestic violence a secret in order to portray the ideal family or keeping someone's sexuality a secret to not upset Grandpa.

**Secrecy breeds more trauma.
Sharing breeds more connection.**

Don't get me wrong, I am not saying yell your trauma stories from the hilltops or post them all over social media like a badge of honor. I am saying, let's stop the repetitive cycle of trauma by communicating it in a psychologically safe environment and a healthy and caring way. Let's disrupt the pattern that says we need to save face so the neighbors don't think badly of us.

Trauma expert and author Dr. Robert Stolorow says that trauma occurs when intense emotional pain cannot find a relational home in which it can be held, borne, and integrated.[12] Essentially, we can't heal from grief, trauma, or chronic stress unless our intense emotional pain finds a home. We do not need to eradicate our trauma, mask it, or numb it to the point of no return. Instead, we must give it a home in which it can be held. I believe we can also do this for other people. Dr. Stolorow has his own words for it. He calls it *emotional dwelling*. Emotional dwelling isn't about empathic understanding but instead means leaning into another's emotional pain and participating in it, "perhaps with aid of one's own analogous experiences of pain."[13]

I love his idea of emotional dwelling, as it's active participation, and real and candid. It's being held in a safe way without covering or masking the trauma. What I didn't realize until recently was that, as a transformational coach myself, I've been innately using a very similar technique and process with my clients during group workshops and retreats. We use the environment to share our souls and actively heal one another of our pain. It's truly an incredible experience.

For example, one of my clients, who we will call Claire, shared her pain about abuse as a child. Instead of simply holding space and listening, the group felt so deeply empathetic to Claire's experience that they leaned into her pain and participated in it. They shared their own stories and held each other in a way that no formal therapy session could. Dwelling together in a safe place allowed Claire to release some of her stored pain.

This wasn't a pity party or a kumbaya moment of pretense; it was simply holding each other in an authentic way to allow the trauma to be seen and passed through. It wasn't a group of "victims" trauma bonding; it was a group of active participants breaking the cycle of trauma together.

When we see two sides of the coin—how generational trauma hurts us and how generational wisdom serves us—we can make peace with its presence in our bodies and minds. I'm not saying this is easy; I'm just saying it's possible.

Stephanie Foo, bestselling author of *What My Bones Know*,

was diagnosed with complex PTSD caused by her own life experiences and inherited trauma from her family history, with her great-grandmother and grandmother surviving the brutal occupation of Malaysia during World War II. She said, "I personally believe that because my great-grandmother and grandmother had to hustle desperately to survive ... that has contributed to the hustle and creativity I've possessed in building my own career and survival skills here in America. It's probably also contributed to my intense anxiety."[14]

I feel similar. My family's proud military attitude contributed to my emotional masking of "sucking it up" and not allowing anything in, but it also gave me the blessing of inheriting a fierce action-taking mindset during crises. Our inherited behaviors can either be blessings or burdens, depending on how we look at them and how they impact our lives.

What are your inherited abilities or patterns?

# Generational Impact Exercise

*What family trauma patterns (spoken or unspoken) are held in your family?*

*How have they affected you and your life?*

......................................................................................................
......................................................................................................
......................................................................................................
......................................................................................................
......................................................................................................
......................................................................................................
......................................................................................................
......................................................................................................

*How have they impacted your worldview or beliefs?*

......................................................................................................
......................................................................................................
......................................................................................................
......................................................................................................
......................................................................................................
......................................................................................................
......................................................................................................
......................................................................................................

*How have they shaped you?*

*What family patterns have been "passed on" in a positive way?*

*What inherited traits have helped you become more resilient or aware?*

*How have you used these inherited traits positively in your life?*

................................................................................
................................................................................
................................................................................
................................................................................
................................................................................
................................................................................
................................................................................
................................................................................
................................................................................
................................................................................
................................................................................
................................................................................
................................................................................
................................................................................
................................................................................
................................................................................

Scan the QR code for a guided meditation to release trauma cycles and embrace those that have served you.

> "Self-mastery requires action. You need to put yourself out there and test your limits."
>
> —NADINE MULLER

CHAPTER 3

# IT'S ALL SELF-MASTERY, REALLY

I could have titled this book *Self-Mastery*, because every single thing discussed is really a lesson in self-mastery. Self-mastery isn't about being a "master" as such; it's really about being a student of life. A lifelong learner who is always on the path to self-mastery.

Now that may sound a little underwhelming to you. Who wants to feel like they're always on the path? I mean, where is destination enlightenment and success, right?

But that's not what I mean. Self-mastery is keeping a beginner's mind even if you have achieved a certain level of success or influence. The Japanese coined the term "beginner's mind";

they call it *shoshin*. *Shoshin* basically means the more you know about a subject and the more "expert" you are, the more likely you are to close your mind to more learning. When you adopt a beginner's mindset, you stay humble and deeply rooted in the present. You engage in the process of learning and growing rather than striving for a static state of perfection (which, for those playing at home, doesn't exist!).

When you embrace your journey and decide to become responsible for it, rather than a victim of it, you are sitting firmly in the saddle of self-mastery. Now, this can feel like you're riding in a wild rodeo at times, but it also means you're taking the reins.

When you get wild and decide to become radically responsible for all that has happened, you step into the arena of self-mastery. And when you do that, you invite a full-blown transformation. You basically change the way you think and behave. You stop dwelling in your victimhood and become a captain of your ship.

When former US president Theodore Roosevelt gave his public address titled "Citizenship in a Republic" to over 25,000 people packed into the streets of Paris on April 23, 1910, he probably didn't realize that it would end up being seen as words of inspiration and comfort to so many modern-day leaders. Leaders from all walks of life have since quoted him and revealed how his speech gave them solace when they were facing big challenges. The title of Brené Brown's bestselling book *Daring Greatly* was inspired by Roosevelt's insight, and Miley Cyrus and

## IT'S ALL SELF-MASTERY, REALLY

Liam Hemsworth even have a portion of his speech tattooed on their bodies. Here's a portion of the speech:

> *It is not the critic who counts: not the man who points out how the strong man stumbles or where the doer of deeds could have done better. The credit belongs to the man who is actually in the arena, whose face is marred by dust and sweat and blood, who strives valiantly, who errs and comes up short again and again, because there is no effort without error or shortcoming, but who knows the great enthusiasms, the great devotions, who spends himself in a worthy cause; who, at the best, knows, in the end, the triumph of high achievement, and who, at the worst, if he fails, at least fails while daring greatly, so that his place shall never be with those cold and timid souls who knew neither victory nor defeat.*[1]

Self-mastery is for the "doer of deeds" and for those who "strive valiantly" and spend their time "in a worthy cause."

Self-mastery is when you DECIDE to:

- Turn your crises into the catalyst
- Stay heart-centered and discerning
- Persist against the odds if required
- Keep to *your* path
- Learn lessons as you go

- Aim for something noble and true
- Pursue your purpose or passion
- Develop insight into yourself
- Develop awareness of your blocks and behaviors
- Remain a perpetual learner of life

The incredible thing about self-mastery is that the moment you engage with the process, life becomes deeper and richer. It's not something external happening to you; you're participating in it as a cocreator.

## Self-Mastery Can Be Learned

Being radically responsible for your own journey can be liberating! You can simply stop blaming others and cease being a victim of the past, and the people in it.

In a nutshell, no one is going to give you what you want. It's up to you to get it.

I was lucky in the fact that my upbringing bred radical responsibility. We were raised like a wolf pack—you belonged to the pack, and you were loved by the pack, but you also had to fend for yourself.

My brother and I recently discussed this, and we both believe that our upbringing is part of the reason why we both hustle (with mastery!) like crazy when we have to. We know that no one is going to do things for us. We took care of ourselves from an early age, and mom and dad often allowed us to do the things that were beyond our age.

The important thing to know is that even if you were raised in a comfortable environment and never had to lift a finger or be responsible for anything or anyone, self-mastery and radical responsibility can be learned. It's a muscle that can be exercised and firmed up. And ... the first step is to dump your victim mindset. Stop blaming the world and the people in it and start accepting that it's up to YOU and only YOU to create change.

You are the man, or the woman, in the arena. Yes, you are!

When I hit rock bottom, paradoxically it gave me the biggest panoramic view of my life. Sure, I had to crawl out by myself, and it was messy and muddy, but the hope of the summit spurred me on. Crawling out of the shit is part of the self-mastery process.

Are we humble enough to get down and do the dirty work to lift ourselves up? Are we able to be seen merely trying? Are we willing to try? Do we have a big enough reason to rise?

Humanistic psychologist Abraham Maslow pioneered a self-mastery movement (which he called self-actualization), and many people loved his hierarchy of needs, so much so that they made it into a pyramid and coined it "Maslow's Hierarchy of Needs."

Maslow believed that we have an innate desire to achieve self-actualization after all our basic needs, such as food, safety, and love have been met. The path to self-actualization is basically the path to reach our full potential. Just before his death in 1970 Maslow expanded his original hierarchy to include three more levels: cognitive, aesthetic, and transcendence needs.[2]

Now, I'm not here to give anyone a lecture on Maslow's

psychological theories, but I also think that we don't have to wait for our needs to be met before we endeavor toward self-actualization. Having our needs met certainly makes it easier, but it doesn't mean it's mandatory. If I had waited for my financial needs to be met, I would never have generated the persistence required to dig myself out of the shithole I had found myself in.

In saying that, I wholeheartedly believe that Maslow's hierarchy of needs outlines our general path of growth and gives us the blueprint for illuminating our journey.

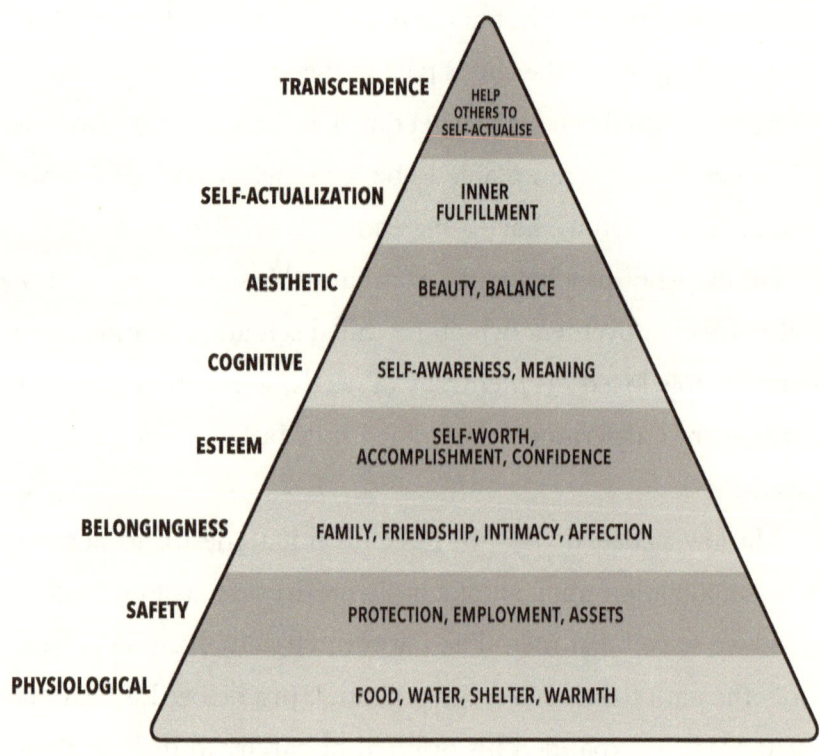

Looking at Maslow's final hierarchy, we can easily identify where we are on the path to self-actualization. It is not a competition, and there is no winner. It is a solo journey of self-mastery.

Self-mastery is a lifelong journey of learning more about our inner world and expressing our unique gifts and talents with the outer world. It's deep and personal work. It's the best journey of your life. But not all choose to take the path toward self-mastery. In fact, it's not glamorous, because it's hard to see. The inner work can also be confronting—overcoming your behaviors, habits of mind, addictions, or aspects of your shadow personality can really test you.

People who show up and do their best to reach their potential are on the road to self-mastery. Of course, not all humans are willing to take this path. Many will balk at it through fear or doubt, reverting back to staying in their comfort zones rather than risking a daring adventure. That's why in my containers, events, workshops, and retreats I always honor and congratulate my clients for turning up! Those who turn up are already on the path; they are in the arena of life ready to discover themselves more fully.

Maslow said: "Self-actualizing people, those who have come to a high level of maturation, health, and self-fulfillment, have so much to teach us that sometimes they seem almost like a different breed of human beings. But, because it is so new, the exploration of the highest reaches of human nature and of its ultimate possibilities and aspirations is a difficult and tortuous task."[3] What I love about this Maslow quote is that he clearly knows that those who take the path of self-mastery are "almost like a different breed of human beings," and yet he also acknowledges that the climb to the summit of possibility and aspiration is "a difficult and tortuous task." He gets it! And that's why we need one another. That's why I love the power and potency of group workshops and retreats—because we all need a tribe who supports our daring adventure toward self-mastery.

Every single thing you do is a gift, an opportunity to master yourself. As the great polymath Leonardo da Vinci stated, "One can have no smaller or greater mastery than mastery of oneself."

## Obstacles Are the Path to Self-Mastery

Now, mastery isn't all about formal learning or degrees. It's a life path. It's much more than an intellectual exercise; it's exercising mastery over your life.

The key to self-mastery is awareness. Becoming aware of yourself. Understanding your mind, emotions, and behaviors. Exercising self-control and paying attention to your impulses and triggers. Understanding how to navigate your life in a way that is authentic and consistent with your true self, your passions, and your purpose.

Self-mastery allows you to drive your life in a way that enables you to live in alignment with your soul.

It sounds damn cliché to say "obstacles are a path to self-mastery"—but it's true. Without the struggles, you can't know yourself. Without being tested, you don't get the chance to draw on

## IT'S ALL SELF-MASTERY, REALLY

your inner resources. You don't know what you're made of.

When I was neck-deep in my holy-fuck life moment, I didn't know if I had the resources to conquer such seemingly insurmountable obstacles. I didn't think I was living a lesson in "self-mastery," and, quite frankly, I didn't care! I just wanted some relief from the pain and struggle.

However, it's only in hindsight that I see that this obstacle was a huge key to my success.

I thought the obstacles were blocking me from achieving my potential ... but they were actually creating me and shaping me into my potential.

They were molding me like a glassmaker moves and twists warm glass in the fire to make art. And much like the phoenix, you only feel the heat of the scorching flames, not realizing in the moment that it's the catalyst for your transformation.

Peace advocate and author Daisaku Ikeda understands that it's through the battle of our lives that self-mastery is gained. He says that we must: "... push open the heavy, groaning doorway of life itself. This is not an easy task. Indeed, it may be the most severely challenging struggle there is. For opening the door to your own life is in the end more difficult than opening the door to all the mysteries of the universe."[4]

It's within life itself that you will find the true keys to your inner transformation. The obstacles can become your greatest opportunities for growth.

Renowned spiritual teacher Paramahansa Yogananda suggested that to attain self-mastery we must learn to control the mind. He said, "The hardest obstacle to overcome is yourself." And, "Your trials did not come to punish you, but to awaken you."

I agree. I discovered that dumping any lasting remnants of a victim mindset allowed me to take radical responsibility for my own life. Seeing obstacles as part of the divine path ensures you don't adopt a "why me?" attitude. Seeing obstacles as opportunities to awaken and RISE is indeed a more empowering lens than seeing yourself as a helpless victim.

This insight is not to be overlooked. If my grandfather had known that his mental obstacles were a symptom of his trauma and not of his weakness, perhaps it could have ended differently for him. If my dad had seen his polio limp as a part of his obstacle toward self-acceptance, he could have acquired inner peace earlier and not spent his life hiding the truth about it.

But we all fall into these traps, right? We see the obstacle or ourselves as the "problem" rather than an opportunity to awaken and head toward further self-mastery.

## Obstacles Exercise

*What are your current challenges or obstacles?*

*What inner resources do they require from you? Is it courage, persistence, endurance, faith, or confidence?*

*If you were to look super hard, are there any small seeds of opportunities for growth within these obstacles? For example, has losing your job allowed you to explore new career avenues? Has losing a relationship opened you up to finding yourself?*

## Awakened Action

Self-mastery requires action. You need to put yourself out there and test your limits.

This doesn't mean doing crazy stunts; it simply means stretching yourself beyond your "normal zone." Challenging yourself forward. Going into uncharted territory. But you don't need to run in headfirst or do what I used to do—take the full-blown warrior attitude and try to conquer everything like a frontline soldier. You can simply lean into self-mastery with awakened action. Awakened action is about choice. Being self-aware enough to make choices that are in alignment with congruent action.

For example, one of my clients, who we will call Rose, always wanted to be a writer. She wrote lots and lots of drafts—she was a champion of perfecting her drafts. She edited them and reedited them. But she never gave those drafts to a publisher or agent. She never got in the actual arena. From the outside, she looked like she was super productive; she looked like she was a writer on a mission. I could tell she was doing a lot of action, but none of it mattered. She was scared to put herself out there. Scared of criticism and rejection. Scared of not being good enough. Sure, she wrote lots of manuscripts; she took writing and editing courses; she went to book clubs and libraries like a groupie, but there was one thing she never did—she never sent her work to a publisher! She never really put herself in the messy arena of intentional action.

This is why procrastination and "being busy" are red flags to me. This is why overworking or being a perfectionist can serve a greater purpose than we might think. On an unconscious level, we often do things that make it look like we're going for our dreams when, in fact, we're avoiding them due to fear of failure.

Awakened action is intentional movement toward your goals and dreams. It is deliberate congruent behavior that matches your intentions.

Without action, we are merely worshiping ideas and thoughts. To make them real and visible, we must follow through.

## The Should Squad

We often know deep in our hearts what we ought to do, but we don't listen. Instead, we listen to all of society's *shoulds* and neglect the YES that lurks deep within our heart. I was a champion of doing the *shoulds*.

I did a job I *should* do for way too long. I did many things I thought I *should* do rather than listen to my inner wisdom. I put myself last because the unconscious paradigm of being a wife and mother meant that's what I *should* do. I soon realized that I was doing all the *shoulds*.

I *should* serve my country.

I *should* be helping people in an emergency department because that's what everyone said I *should* do.

I *should* be getting up at stupid-o'clock and be away from my kids in order to get more, have more, and be more.

In order to get ahead, I *should* grind even harder.

I realized that, at the bottom end of all this shoulding, I was actually living outside of my own value system, doing the opposite of what I wanted for myself.

This happened everywhere. It's part of our toxic conditioning. It's not just women either; men face it too. I first saw it in Dane when his mental health started showing its cracks, and we see it in all the men who come to our retreats too. They're living with a whole bunch of shoulds.

I *should* be strong.

I *should* provide lots of money.

I *should* not be crying.

I *should* not show weakness.

I *should* not be having suicidal thoughts.

I *should* be more capable.

Doing all the *shoulds* means we often don't do what we must. In order to live an awakened life, we must reassess the *shoulds* and reinvestigate the musts. Musts are what your soul is here to do. Your unique mission. Your purpose and pursuit.

We must disrupt the social paradigm of shoulding ourselves to death. Life is not a checklist of boxes that must be ticked by society's arbitrary standards. It's not what will make you happy. In fact, it may be the very thing making you miserable.

When my hubby and I decided to sell our house, our belongings, take the kids out of school, and hit the road in an RV with two kids and a dog, you can imagine how many people thought we were nuts! Of course, there were some awesome cheerleaders too, but I remember people saying, "Oh, the kids will live like Gypsies ... who will educate them?" Or, "I wish I was lucky like you and could do that ... but I can't because we have jobs and a mortgage, blah blah blah."

Well ... guess what? Anyone can do what the hell they want. It's a radical act of courage, self-love, and a course in self-mastery to live the life of your dreams. As author Brianna West says, "The greatest act of self-love is to no longer accept a life you are unhappy with."

**Awakened action is all about taking steps that challenge you TOWARD your desired outcomes. It's about being deliberate and conscious and congruent with your actions.**

Aviation pioneer and trailblazer for women's rights Amelia Earhart was the first woman to fly solo across the Atlantic Ocean (and the second person to do it). She knew that it takes more than mere thinking about something to make it a reality; it takes action. She often spoke about the need to "just do it" before Nike ever did. That's what pioneering something takes ... awakened and inspired action in the direction of your dreams.

> *"There is more to life than being a passenger."*
> **—AMELIA EARHART**

## Awakened Action Exercise

*What is one tiny thing you could do within the next twenty-four hours that would take you a step closer to a goal or outcome you desire? It could be to finish your résumé, make that call about a course you've been putting off, or organize a date with your partner. It could be to send that email about vacancies for volunteer work—anything that will take you a tiny step closer to your goal.*

*What is one bigger action you could take within the next week that would take you a step closer to a goal or outcome you desire?*

..................................................................................................

..................................................................................................

..................................................................................................

..................................................................................................

..................................................................................................

..................................................................................................

..................................................................................................

*What small action could you take that's out of your comfort zone and that you know you need to take? When will you take it by (be specific with a date)?*

..................................................................................................

..................................................................................................

..................................................................................................

..................................................................................................

..................................................................................................

..................................................................................................

..................................................................................................

*What are some actions you have taken within the past year that were in alignment with your desired outcomes?*

## Get Behind Yourself and Use Teflon

Backing yourself isn't just a cliché—it takes grit. Backing yourself is a step toward mastering yourself and your emotions. Be there for yourself, even if, *especially* if, no one else is.

Now, as women we are wayyyy more used to criticizing ourselves and putting ourselves down instead of boosting ourselves up and backing ourselves. I don't know about you, but I'm tired of that old paradigm. Backing yourself means you'll support yourself, you'll be a cheerleader of yourself instead of a criticizer, you'll say encouraging things to yourself, you'll believe in your own abilities. You'll hold yourself compassionately during tough times and talk to yourself tenderly.

I often tell my clients that self-mastery also involves dealing with criticism and judgment. It seems to be especially targeted to those who unapologetically follow their dreams. I like to remind people to Teflon themselves. Teflon, of course, is that substance that nothing sticks to in pots and pans. So if someone launches horse shit at you (in the form of criticism or judgment), you can let the Teflon protect you, and the shit slides right off. Now that, of course, can be easier said than done, but with practice it's possible to add a layer of skin as a boundary that makes others' opinions slide right off you. You no longer have to let shit stick to you. You no longer have to stink.

There is an old Buddhist scripture that sums up Teflon perfectly.

One day, Buddha was visiting a village, and a very angry and rude young man had been taunting him for hours and hours.

"You have no right teaching others," the man shouted. "You are nothing but a fake!"

Buddha was not worried by this man's continual insults.

Instead, after a period of time, Buddha asked the young man, "If I buy a gift and offer it to you, but you do not accept the gift, then to whom does the gift belong?"

The young man paused, a little shocked by the question. He said, "It would belong to you, because you bought the gift."

Buddha smiled. "That is correct," he said. "And it is exactly the same with your anger. If you become angry with me and I do not get insulted, then the anger falls back on you. You are then the only one who becomes unhappy, not me. All you have done is hurt yourself."

That is mastery!

Now, of course, none of us are Buddha! But we all have the nature within us, and, in dealing with external critics, we can simply *not* accept the "gifts" of criticism, judgment, and opinions flung at us.

So, besides growing a new Teflon skin, how can you back yourself? It takes knowledge of your values. How can you really master yourself if you don't know your values? It's hard. But knowing what matters to you when all else falls away is a form of mastery.

## Know Your Values

Your values are the things that are important to you. They help you prioritize your life and determine how you spend your time.

When you define your values and commit to living them, you immediately set a new standard of living. You become congruent. When the things you do and the way you behave match your core values, life is simplified and electric! Your energy rises, and you no longer spend time on shit you don't value, meaning more time for the things that *are* important to you.

Not knowing your values usually sets you up to simply bubbling along, going with the flow of others' values. It doesn't mean you're living wrongly; it just means you aren't connected to what really matters to *you*—uniquely to you.

Your values are the foundation of your choices, your actions, and your behaviors. When you know your core values, it's like having your very own Ten Commandments—they act as your rudder for living rightly. Not knowing your values can lead you into trouble. As Miss Grace Reavy, US advocate for the National Women's Party, suggested as a slogan back in 1946, "Unless you stand for something, you'll fall for anything."

When we are aligned with our values, it gives rise to the best version of ourselves, setting the standards for our lives, careers, and relationships.

Before I ask you to define your values, I'll share mine:

- Health
- Love
- Family
- Freedom
- Service
- Generosity
- Leadership
- Courage

## Live in Alignment with Your Values

I often challenge my clients when they first declare their values. For example, if your top value is family, are you spending time with them? Or are you always working or pursuing other interests? If you value honesty, are you always honest? Or do you allow yourself to get away with little white lies? Why do we sometimes compromise our own set of values? Well, while some people like the idea of a certain value, they don't necessarily want to put effort into living it. Defining your values is one thing. Living them takes conscious effort.

So, the question for you is: **are you living in alignment with your values?**

Living your values is one of the foundational steps of self-mastery. It cannot be skipped or neglected.

One of our clients, who we will call Tim, announced in one of our workshops that his top value was family. I challenged him on that. He was working so many hours that he rarely saw his family. While he valued them 100 percent—he worked for them; they were his driving force—he wasn't living in alignment with his values. His values weren't fully displayed in action. By providing for them, he was somewhat living his family value, but to fully live it he needed to show them that he valued spending quality time with them. With connection.

Now, Tim couldn't easily change his work situation. He was the main breadwinner, and his family needed him to pay the mortgage and fund the kids' education. But that didn't mean he couldn't live congruently with his values. We encouraged him to carve out some special one-to-one time with each family member (including his partner) on the weekends. One family member every weekend, and some group family time like a movie together or a special lunch or dinner. Tim followed our advice, and his whole life changed. The kids felt more valued than ever before, and his wife fell more in love with him. He didn't change his work hours; he changed his free time. Instead of bumbling around aimlessly on the weekends, he was intentional! He showed his family that he cared and that he valued each person uniquely. For Tim, it was a game changer.

## Values Exercise

*Write down your top eight values.*

*Write down the actions/behaviors that align with each value.*

*Write down the actions/behaviors that misalign with each value.*

*Example:*

| VALUES | ALIGNED ACTION | MISALIGNED ACTION |
|---|---|---|
| Honesty | Truth telling | Half-truths/deception |
| Family | Putting family first<br>Quality time with family | Workaholism |

| VALUES | ALIGNED ACTION | MISALIGNED ACTION |
|---|---|---|
|  |  |  |
|  |  |  |
|  |  |  |
|  |  |  |
|  |  |  |
|  |  |  |
|  |  |  |
|  |  |  |

\* Check out a list of values on the next page to kickstart your values exercise.

| | | | |
|---|---|---|---|
| Acceptance | Drive | Loyalty | Restraint |
| Accomplishment | Eagerness | Motivation | Results-Oriented |
| Accountability | Education | Objectivity | Reverence |
| Adaptability | Effectiveness | Openness | Satisfaction |
| Adventurous | Endurance | Optimism | Security |
| Agility | Energetic | Organisation | Sensitivity |
| Altruism | Enthusiasm | Originality | Serenity |
| Ambition | Equality | Passion | Seriousness |
| Authenticity | Excellence | Patience | Simplicity |
| Balance | Experience | Peace | Skillfulness |
| Beauty | Fairness | Perceptiveness | Spontaneity |
| Boldness | Fearlessness | Performance | Stability |
| Bravery | Focused | Persistence | Strength |
| Caring | Forthright | Persuasion | Success |
| Certainty | Generosity | Philanthropy | Support |
| Charisma | Gratitude | Poise | Sustainability |
| Charity | Growth | Positive | Synergy |
| Cleverness | Guidance | Power | Talent |
| Commitment | Honesty | Precision | Teamwork |
| Communication | Hospitality | Productivity | Thoroughness |
| Compassion | Humility | Professionalism | Tolerance |
| Confidence | Imagination | Profitability | Toughness |
| Consistency | Impact | Progress | Training |
| Courage | Influence | Prosperity | Transparency |
| Creativity | Ingenuity | Punctuality | Trustworthiness |
| Curiosity | Innovation | Purpose | Truth |
| Daring | Inspiration | Qualified | Uniqueness |
| Decisiveness | Integrity | Quality | Unity |
| Dependability | Intelligence | Quick-minded | Variety |
| Directness | Interdependence | Reliability | Virtue |
| Discernment | Justice | Resilience | Vision |
| Discipline | Kindness | Resourcefulness | Wealth |
| Discretion | Knowledge | Respect | Wellness |
| Diversity | Leadership | Responsibility | Wisdom |

## Reflections
*Are you living congruent to your values?*
*Which values are aligned?*
*Which values are misaligned?*


**Note:** Your values shift over time. What you valued at thirteen won't be the same as what you value at thirty. As you evolve and change into another version of yourself, so do your values shift.

# Who Are You Behind the Labels?

During my workshops and retreats, one of the most powerful ah-ha moments people have is when they tap into their authentic self. This is when they discover who they are behind all the masks and labels.

You are more than just your occupation or marital status. You are more than your ethnicity or religious persuasion. You are more than a mother, wife, sister, daughter, or husband, dad, brother, or son. You are far greater than any labels people give you, or the ones you give yourself.

Now, of course, some labels can be very fulfilling and positive for people's identity. For example, a positive label may be: I am an activist; I am a teacher; I am a mother of plenty; I am a vegan; I am a Christian; I am a badass creative movie director. A positive label you love can feel super-duper empowering and can boost confidence.

Yet people change, and so do labels. One day, you might be a lawyer, and a few years later you might be a retiree who loves to frolic in paint-by-numbers. You might be a model, and then a mom, and then a modeling mom who advocates for self-love and brings awareness to postnatal depression. You might be a bodybuilding vegan and then suffer a career crisis and become a self-development coach.

Your labels change and grow, but your authentic self is always static. Your authentic self lies behind all the labels and never shape-shifts. It doesn't worry about occupations and titles or accomplishments and failures.

Your authentic self is your truest and most natural inner essence. It's the deep inner you that *knows*. It's the one who witnesses all the experiences and moods "you" have. It witnesses all the struggles and triumphs. Your authentic self is a spiritual part of you. It is more than your personality. Yet it's not hidden from the world—it's the force that animates your mind, body, and its expression. It's the part of you that has access to wisdom, intuition, and knowing without knowing how you know.

When you tap into your authentic self, you get to know the inner you behind all the labels people think define you.

When you live congruently with your authentic self, life becomes a journey of self-mastery. You become freer because you don't feel the need to live up to other people's labels for you. Nor do you feel that you need a list of labels and titles to be accepted. You get to know your authentic self, and life becomes richer. As Oprah said, "I had no idea that being your authentic self could make me as rich as I've become. If I had, I'd have done it a lot earlier."

To discover your authentic self, download this free meditation and come on a journey with me into the deeper recesses of your soul.

 Scan the QR code for a guided visualization to meet your authentic higher self.

> "The authentic self is soul made visible."
> —SARAH BAN BREATHNACH

## Your Future Self

When you discover your authentic self, you can become intentional about who you are and what you're here to do. You can also tap into your "future self" and begin to manifest your authentic self through life experiences and events.

My entire business is now built around my authentic self. It is built around my two children, my husband, and all the amazing women, men, couples, and families I am honored to mentor, lead, and serve.

Famous Swedish psychologist Carl Jung suggested that your future self already exists and it's trying to manifest in the present. He suggests that it's trying to draw your attention to things of interest to you and fill your consciousness with signs, symbols, and synchronicities to help you awaken and manifest your highest potential.

You see, becoming conscious of your highest self helps you RISE. It automatically escalates you to a higher way of thinking about yourself and your existence.

# Who Are You Now?

*So where are you now? What is important to you right now?*

*What is your future self trying to manifest through you and into the world?*

..................................................................................................
..................................................................................................
..................................................................................................
..................................................................................................
..................................................................................................
..................................................................................................
..................................................................................................

*What comes naturally to you?*

..................................................................................................
..................................................................................................
..................................................................................................
..................................................................................................
..................................................................................................
..................................................................................................
..................................................................................................

*What unique talents and gifts can you offer the world?*

*What is your highest service to others?*

You don't need all the answers to these questions in one massive moment of realization. Let it trickle out of your consciousness through reflection and observation. I often find that journaling this type of thing can be super helpful. It is useful to become adept at identifying your authentic self versus the shoulds and obligations imposed on you.

## Journal Power

I believe in the power of journaling. It helps you reflect, be intentional, and notice patterns of behavior and thought. Journaling can be an easy way to see your progress and your cyclic challenges.

You can journal about your past, your present, and your future. You can write about your hopes, your dreams, your fears, and your successes.

An incredible study from *Psychosomatic Medicine* found that expressive writing can help us heal faster. Researchers asked healthy adults between the ages of 64 and 97 to journal a mere three days in a row for 20 minutes a day. Half the groups were asked to write about things that upset them and to journal their honest thoughts and feelings. The other half wrote about how they manage their time during the day. A couple of weeks later, all participants had a tiny biopsy performed on their arms, resulting in a small wound. Researchers tracked how the wounds healed by taking a picture every day. A huge 76 percent of the group who voiced their upsetting thoughts and feelings healed quickly compared to 42 percent who wrote about time management.[5]

But journaling doesn't just work for expressing upsetting thoughts. It also helps us recognize good things and express them. Studies show that keeping a gratitude journal can enhance our mood, help with our mental health, and ease anxiety and depressive episodes.[6]

It seems that using a journal helps our brains process trauma and joy and make sense of our experiences. Studies reveal that keeping a journal that has personal emotional meaning and expression is key.

## Notice Signs and Synchronicities

I also suggest to my clients to stay attuned to signs and synchronicities during the process of self-discovery and self-mastery. The signs help you know that you're on the right path. That you're in communication with the universe and its plan for you.

You do have all the answers within, in your personal relationship with Source.

When you're looking for direction, the truth is, YOU ARE THE COMPASS. The universe will conspire with your needs and wishes if they are authentic. You can master your mind, your emotions, your body, your wealth, your relationships, your parenting, your life. You can steer the compass of life to your highest self. This is not false hope, but bona fide truth. You are the answer to your prayers, and along the road to self-mastery, it will be the final answer. It is always up to you! No one can conquer your mind, problems, or dreams for you.

If you're silently waiting around for some knight in shining armor to relieve you of all your insecurities and anxieties, then grab a ticket to the longest queue in the world. Lots of people are waiting for the same savior. But if you're willing to risk yourself, rely on yourself, and back yourself, then you build an entirely new relationship with yourself and others—a thriving, flourishing, and mature relationship based on courage. As author Kerry E. Wagner said, "You don't have to worry about burning bridges, if you're building your own."

Yes! Build your own fucking bridge and dance over it.

CHAPTER 4

# TAKE THE DIRECT PATH

If you really want to RISE, like ... not just RISE but freakin' soar like a jet engine ... there's an easier way than the good ol' hustle and grind. Yep, there's a direct path! Now, I must confess that taking the direct path didn't come naturally to me. It took a while for me to get over my Miss-Hyper-Independence-and-I-can-do-everything-myself attitude. It took me a little while to see and understand there *really* is a slipstream to success. And now ... I'm a total convert. Hallelujah and amen!

Now, I'm not saying you won't be challenged and it's all rainbows and ponies on the good ship lollipop. I guarantee 100 percent that you will be challenged, no doubt about it. But I also guarantee that you'll reach your dreams much quicker. It's a sure thing.

Taking the road to success comes with a couple of options: A) you can take the long road (repetitive learning through endless cycles of pain) or B) you can take the slipstream and learn from people who have traveled before you. I'm talking about the transformative power of great mentors and coaches.

Now, before you roll your eyes and think, *Oh, another coach banging on about the power of coaching*—hear me out. You see, as you know, I was hyper-independent, and my brain was programmed to do all things by myself. I was hell-bent on relying solely on me, myself, and I. Even though I still believe we must all be radically responsible for our own lives, it doesn't mean we must do everything alone. I mean, we don't even arrive on Planet Earth on our own … so why do we think we must fly solo when we're here?

It took me a while to arrive at this junction. When a discussion about coaches or mentors came up, my brain would always think, *I don't need anybody's help … If I got myself into this mess, then I can get myself out. How could someone who doesn't even know me possibly help me?*

I had zero interest in having a coach or mentor and zero interest in being coached. I was your typical alpha female—prowling around my own territory on hyperalert, looking to defend myself or act on my own terms. I thought that needing help somehow revealed a weakness and meant I was incapable of gaining success on my own. Now, yes—I was raised in a self-reliant environment, and my military programming was strong! Even as a critical-care-trained nurse, I was trained to take care of others and not think of myself. However, being a lone wolf often worked well for me, and I wasn't keen to change it! I saw it as a superpower and took the "if it ain't broken, why fix it?" approach. Why look for a coach or a mentor if I was already A-OK, right?

## My Circus Act Confession

Funnily enough, it never occurred to me that the best business leaders, the best athletes, the wisest spiritual teachers, and even the best writers mostly all had a coach or mentor (or several). In hindsight, I can clearly see that my aversion to having a coach or mentor was a form of internal warfare with myself. I was battling my internal narratives, creating stories about what having a coach or mentor meant, none of which were technically true, but I didn't care. I made getting help mean that I wasn't capable enough, good enough, competent enough to get everything I required done.

Somewhere in my warped sense of reality, I was supposed to build a business empire while being a loving and connected homeschooling mother of two, with ample time for my husband and kids, while keeping fit, healthy, and on top of my game 100 percent of the time on all levels—physical, mental, emotional, and spiritual—without a shred of help from outside sources. Yep, that was my game plan. The problem with that approach was it took a ridiculous amount of time, effort, and loss of sleep (and sanity) to execute. It meant that I had to run around like a wild woman, juggling too many awkward obstacles in an attempt to keep everything functioning. One little hiccup, and my entire schedule could malfunction. It was like watching a bad circus act—imagine a trapeze artist wearing a blindfold and trying to juggle fire torches while still smiling like everything is working perfectly. Well, that was me. Sound familiar?

So there I was, attempting the impossible juggling act, determined to do everything at the highest standard. I didn't realize this type of extreme act was destined for imminent disaster. After all, what could possibly go wrong?

Of course, I was blinded to this. I could not see I was on a road to exhaustion and burnout. I just figured, if I kept up my heroic acts, then it would all turn out OK. All the motivational leaders are built on this same hustle and grind culture, right? So, to me, this was the sacrifice and price worth paying to make all my dreams come true.

And it worked. For a short while, anyway. It wasn't until I tried to perform all the roles in my own business that I realized something had to change. That something was *me*. I was the common denominator. The curtains had to close on my juggling act.

But I simply couldn't let go of the reins. I felt I needed to be everything in my business—the director, the salesperson, the accountant, the mentor, the marketing leader, the social media guru, the meeting coordinator, the events manager, and whatever other roles we required. I had a vision of the business, and I could clearly see what we needed to succeed. The problem was, because I was the visionary, I felt that I could do all the jobs in alignment with the vision better than anyone else. After all, it was my vision, so I kinda had some inside information no one else was privy to. Finally, I got the rude awakening I needed.

I simply could not grow my vision while taking on all those roles. Damn! Checkmate. I was thrust into a corner with limited options, and my old way of doing things was no longer working. In fact, I was exhausting myself and pissing off anyone who tried to help. But letting go didn't come naturally to me. I was like a screaming child whose mother is trying to head out the door to go to work but can't because the child is wrapped around her leg yelling, "Don't go! Stay here."

Letting go was something I had to learn. Much like that screaming child has to learn that their mother will come home, I had to learn that my business will prosper if I trust others to help. Gulp. *Could I do that?*

At first, I was terrible. I sucked at taking a step back. I was feigning "letting go" but was really just micromanaging people with the illusion that I was relaxing my deep need for control. I was convincing myself that I was empowering others within the business, but when it came to important decisions, I stepped in and took over. I couldn't let a mistake be made. My business was too important to me. Sure, I was getting better and allowing others to make unimportant decisions but could not and would not allow others to make major decisions.

Every big decision was made by me. The problem was ... the very thing that made me successful—my hyper-independent go-getting attitude—was now getting in the way and impeding my growth.

Previous to this awakening, I was making all the business decisions, mostly through trial and error. But as the business grew, I was facing more and more decisions I had never dealt with before, which meant some of my decisions were simply "best guesses." My business was growing, but I was losing precious time, money, and energy taking the trial-and-error approach. It became clear that I needed guidance; I needed to bounce ideas off people who had been there and done that.

For quite possibly the first time in my life, I didn't want to figure everything out on my own. I knew I needed help.

## Getting Out of Your Own Way

Often, the first step to getting ahead is getting out of your own way. We rarely see ourselves as the obstacle, but quite often we are. It could be our lack of self-belief, our procrastination, our perfectionism, low self-worth, caring what other people think, fear, or mental programming that becomes an obstacle in our path.

For me, it was my hyper-independence and inability to let others help. My programming said things that weren't factually true but my brain deemed true for me. Things like:

*If I want something to be done well, I must do it myself.*
*Getting help is a sign of weakness.*
*Coaches probably just want my money.*
*Mentors are for huge global-level business executives.*
*Who can possibly help me if they don't know me?*

*I don't need someone's actual help. I can learn everything through books and videos.*

*I have business friends who I can talk to. Why pay someone?*

You see, hyper-independence can show up as a strength when it's really masquerading as a shadow. It can start from the survival instinct we inherently have—the need to survive trauma or look after ourselves. It can also appear in some individuals and subcultures more deeply than others. I have coached many women from a variety of cultures, and quite often hyper-independence appears when they need to look after themselves from an early age because both parents were working insane hours just to educate them and put food on the table. Or when they had one parent working around the clock and the kids had to become a "mini parent" from a very early age.

Naturally, self-reliance is a remarkable skill to have. It's essential to be able to take responsibility and rely on your amazing self. However, we must also be willing to see it as a double-edged sword. Every light casts a shadow.

Late author Dr. Wayne Dyer told countless people that he saw his childhood circumstances as God's gift. He was raised in an orphanage with his brothers, and he believed that being an orphan was his golden path to learn self-reliance so he could teach it to others. He also said because his mission was to teach self-reliance, God said to Wayne before he entered the world, "Well, then, we'd better get your little ass into an orphanage."[1] Therefore, his experience was in perfect alignment with his destiny.

For me, looking at this shadow part of myself was tough. It meant facing my ugly fears and seeing how they masqueraded as control. If I didn't control things, then I worried they would fall apart or wouldn't happen the way I wanted them to.

Growing up with a massive amount of space and independence meant my brother and I ran our own lives from an early age. We had to be independent. We handled our school schedules and spent lots of time without parental supervision. For us, this was normal; we didn't expect our parents to cut the crust off our sandwiches or dote on us like other parents. We knew that our parents loved us dearly, but we also knew they parented *very* differently from the typical sitcom-style family life. Hyper-independence was a way of life for us.

Social psychologists define some common characteristics of hyper-independence and how they can easily prevent you from seeking help or acquiring coaching or support from others. You may recognize some red flags here … but don't worry—there's no judgment. I ticked all the boxes, and it's rather surprising I didn't end up becoming a dominatrix! Just kidding.

### Common Characteristics of Hyper-Independence
- Taking on too much (over and over again)
- Not trusting others to do the job or task to your standards
- Saying no to help
- Difficulty in delegating tasks
- Refusing to ask for help and instead taking extreme action to cope

- Often busy and burdened with tasks but refuse to share the burden
- Can exhibit workaholic tendencies
- Finding it difficult to show vulnerability or admit struggle
- Extreme feelings of guilt if anyone does help, or if you ask for a small favor
- Feeling obligated to pay back any small gesture or gift

You see, sometimes our strengths are so strong that we insist we must keep them just as they are. We don't see them as inhibitors or obstacles, even when they are. We don't have to *give up* our strengths. On the contrary. We can simply adjust them and allow some wiggle room to invite something new into the mix. For example, I have never relinquished my need to be hyper-independent—no way! What I did was give it balance. I adjusted my hyper-independence to allow some space for others to enter. This meant I had to shut up sometimes. I had to train my staff rather than do things myself. I had to empower my team to make decisions, and I had to get a coach to help me with my blind spots and my incessant need to do everything myself.

When I spoke to fellow entrepreneurs about business, they all seemed so ridiculously comfortable with having mentors or coaches. In fact, I was a little bit tired of constantly hearing, "My coach says … [insert some epic wisdom here]." They all marveled at what a difference a coach or mentor had made in their lives. After hearing this for years and seeing many of my colleagues' businesses go gangbusters, I figured maybe there was something to this coaching and mentoring hype they'd been banging on about.

So guess what I did? It's kinda obvious, hey? Yep, I went and got myself my first-ever coach (cue the epic soundtrack now as I walk off into the sunset).

## What's Stopping You from Seeking a Good Coach or Mentor?

So if you're someone who wants to level up and take the rocket ship to Planet Success, then it's wise to take a raw reality check and see what's standing in your way. Is it you?

The next question is—do you have someone reputable and experienced who can accelerate your journey? Do you have someone in your corner who has "been there and done that" helping you succeed? If you do, then bravo! Well done to you. I trust you're getting results. (Actually, side note: I *insist* you're getting results).

If you don't have someone helping you, then what is preventing you?

There are many legit reasons why people haven't got a coach or mentor yet. There are also countless excuses. Let's look at the ones I often see or hear ...

### ～ "I'm not ready yet."

Some people insist they're not ready for a coach or mentor. They first need to have a certain level of success or have some sort of order in their business or personal life. This is a big fat myth! The best time to get help is when you need it, not when you are on holiday in the Bahamas sipping martinis. No one is too inexperienced or too small of an entrepreneur to get guidance. If you want to grow—then don't wait. Get support in place early, and you will shed off years of trying and effort. The biggest regret I have about having a coach is that I didn't get one sooner.

If you feel you're not emotionally ready to dive in, then just dip your toe in a little. Incremental steps are still progress. In fact, some incredibly successful and happy people have built their entire career and life on taking small steps often. BJ Fogg, a research scientist who runs a behavior design lab at Stanford University, built an entire movement based on the power of tiny incremental steps to help people achieve their best life.

I guess this is age-old advice ... As Confucius said, "The man who moves a mountain begins by carrying away small stones." Or Lao Tzu's famous quote—"A journey of a thousand miles begins with a single step."

So why are these quotes still plastered everywhere in modern times? Because they're true! They haven't gone out of fashion, because we still need to hear their wisdom.

Just because you're not ready yet, it doesn't mean you can't start with a single step, no matter how tiny.

## ᗛ "When I get this or that done, I will get a coach."

Perfectionism is a sly little beast; it can rear its ugly head in ways that often appear as logic. For example, I have heard people say, *When I hire a PA, I will get a coach. When I employ more people, I will get a coach. When I decide to really go for my dreams, I will get a coach. When I finish my course, my exams, my book, my online course, my degree*—then *I will hire a coach.*

Often, we delay that moment we erroneously believe we need to reach to feel worthy of a coach. Or we believe we need to have certain things done and ticked off our list to start living our BIG life (you know, the one we feel we're meant to live).

This type of delay is frequently due to a deeper level of perfectionism and procrastination. Often unconsciously, we don't want to be accountable to our dreams. We can fear facing them. We can fear what they may interrupt in our life. What they may stir up in our perfect little bubble. They may challenge us to take a risk.

Yes, you'll be surprised to know how many clients I've had to push through the fear of success. The fear of facing their deepest desires and going for them. It's bloody confronting! Seriously.

So delaying a coach or saying, *"One day* I will get a coach" is often an unconscious mechanism trying to keep you safe. Because let's be frank—following your dreams is a wild ride, and we know what happens when you hire a good coach … Yep, they hold you to account! They reflect back your blind spots, draw out your dreams, and hold them up in front of your face to be seen and acted upon. Delaying this accountability is a surefire way to never have to face it. So we use the illusion of perfectionism (needing everything perfect before we hire a coach), or we procrastinate (delay the moment from happening).

Ahhh our minds are so incredibly brilliant; the psyche can even hide things from our waking level of consciousness.

> *"One day or day one. You decide."*
> —PAULO COELHO

### ↭ "I know what I'm doing" or "I can do this myself."

Wow! I can speak as an expert on this one. The whole "I know what I'm doing, so I don't need a coach" caper is a defense mechanism. Often, capable self-reliant people feel they don't need someone outside to help. They can perceive it as a weakness of their character or abilities. They feel an overwhelming sense of responsibility to handle their own affairs.

This trait can appear when people have been hurt in the past and don't trust others easily. Or they have had to rely on themselves from an early age and don't know how to rely on others very well. They don't trust easily, so they refuse any help offered. This could be to avoid an inevitable confrontation. For example, if others don't meet their standards or expectations, instead of trying to work with someone, they avoid it. This is a means to avoid confrontation and avoid feeling bad.

My colleague, Zoe, did this often. She needed to hire a mentor for her fashion business but was very certain she knew what to do. Zoe wanted to grow her business internationally, but there was just one little problem—she had never had an international brand. Like *never*! When I suggested that she needed to find someone doing exactly what she wanted to do, and get mentoring, she scoffed at me.

"They may work differently to me," she said.

"Yes, they may," I said, "but they are already succeeding in the precise area you want to succeed in. They already know some things you don't."

"I'll figure it out myself," she insisted. "That's how I built my company in the first place."

When we drilled into her fears about getting some advice from someone already succeeding in her industry, it became clear that she wasn't scared to grow her business; she wasn't scared to invest money in a good coach, or even learn some new things. She was scared of her own expectations. You see, Zoe had high standards, and she wouldn't compromise them, because that's what made her brand successful. She was worried that the coach wouldn't meet her high expectations, and then she would have to be honest with them and be disappointed it didn't work out. She would end up having to let them down. She had been in this position too many times, and it always made her uncomfortable, so … she avoided it before it even happened. Problem solved.

She didn't want to be disappointed. She didn't want another failed partnership due to the coach not being as good as she wanted. She didn't want the awkward situation where she had to confront them or discontinue the relationship.

When I reflected back to her that she was avoiding disappointment through not trying, she laughed. Lightbulb moment. She could see her pattern. Now, I didn't ask Zoe to lower her expectations, as that would be poor advice. Instead, I asked her if she would consider hiring the absolute best she could find and letting them know up front about her aversion to being coached and why. If Zoe's experience matches your own, explain your fears to any potential coach up front. Simply say, "My main concern about having a coach is that my high standards will be difficult to meet and we may both be left feeling disappointed from the experience. I don't know how to work with this … What do you suggest we do?" A good coach will take this as a beautiful invitation, and the real coaching will start then and there.

Spoiler alert—Zoe did get coached. She found her match. She did lots and lots of research and didn't just hire anyone. She hired an incredible mentor who drew the lines of engagement early, challenged her, and supported her unique vision. She went international and launched a new range (that was her coach's advice, launch a new range, and it worked). She changed her mind about coaching. I know that humbling feeling.

## ~ "How could someone who doesn't know me possibly help me?"

It's true. It does feel weird to think a stranger could help you with something personal, whether that is your own personal issues or your business or parenting concerns. It was a big block for me at first.

But let me ask you this ... if you want a surgeon to operate on you, would you insist they know you? Or would you insist they know their job? What is more personal than having someone perform surgery on your one-and-only body! How intimate, right?

What about a dentist? What about a beautician? Or an electrician?

You see being an expert coach doesn't mean you need to know every single detail about someone. It's not therapy. It's about doing certain actions to achieve a certain result, and, along the way, there are plenty of notorious pitfalls and obstacles set to challenge you.

Edmund Hillary was celebrated as the first person to reach the summit of Mount Everest. But was he? Ever heard of Tenzing Norgay? Well ... Tenzing was the Nepalese-Indian Sherpa and Hillary's teammate. He had made many expeditions to Mount Everest before Hillary, but the teams he ventured with had never made it to the summit. Norgay and Hillary both made it to the summit that day. In fact, Hillary even credits Norgay with saving his life. But as history would have it, Hillary was knighted by the Queen and given the accolades as the first person to reach the summit, while Norgay was given a medal and often left out of the media headlines.

You see, Edmund Hillary needed an experienced Sherpa if he had even the slightest chance of making it up the hill. He didn't need Norgay to know his every thought, but he did need someone he could rely on, someone who knew how to climb a treacherous mountain against all odds. Someone who had the most experience at doing something so radical. That man was Tenzing.

Without Tenzing's experience, there was no way that Edmund Hilary would be revered in our modern history books. See where I'm going here?

Now, don't get me wrong—it's essential that a coach knows you and understands your challenges. But hiring them based on the lie – *how could someone I don't know possibly help me?* — is flawed thinking. There is nothing more helpful than experience-based advice by someone who has succeeded in the industry or area you want to succeed in.

Even Buddha's spiritual seekers came up with this same argument. Why does one need a teacher? Because Buddha was so wise, he taught in parables and stories that made sense to his students.

Here's one of Buddha's parables …

One day, a man was traveling alone and came to a big river. There was no way to cross the river, and he was stranded and didn't know what to do. With no other way to cross the huge expanse of water, he decided to grab some branches, creeper vines, and reeds and create a raft.

It took some time, but eventually the man constructed a makeshift raft that could float. He used his hands and legs as paddles and got himself to the other side. He could then take the next step in his journey.

Buddha asked his students, "Now, once he got across the water, what would he do with the raft? Would he carry it along or drag it behind him because it served him well? No, he would drop the raft because he no longer needed it."

"My teachings [the dharma] are the raft. They are useful for transporting you to the other side but not to hold onto."

What a wise one, hey? Good coaches, mentors, and teachers are a raft! They will get you to the other side of the river, but you must paddle.

## ∾ "I can't ask for help."

Worrying about asking for help is an obstacle for many women. We have been sold an illusion that suggests modern-day women must be superheroes. I do, in fact, meet many superhero women—they are my tribe. But the thing is, there's a ridiculous culture often unspoken by women that unconsciously says we must do everything amazingly to be deemed "worthy." I call bullshit! Not asking for help is like a parasite leeching the best vitamins from you. Without help, we become sucked dry, burnt out, exhausted, and resentful. And then we feel guilty for being cranky, right?

A recent report reveals that nearly half (48 percent) of

18-to-29-year-olds say they feel drained and exhausted. Forty percent of people aged 30 and up say the same, and, on average, women had much higher levels of burnout than men. Over 46 percent of women suffer burnout compared to 37 percent of men.[2]

I don't know about you, but something isn't right in our feminine world. These stats are ballistic! Nearly half of the feminine power in this world is drained AF or burnt out and wanting to just lie on the couch and watch Netflix so we can recover from the grind of our mad world.

I wonder if our culture of not asking for help has anything to do with it. You see, women these days are taking on a lot, and I mean A LOT! We're raising families, building empires, taking care of others, keeping friendship circles, and trying to do it all flawlessly. There's just one teeny-weeny issue with our awesomeness ... We are trying to do it all solo. Even if we have a loving partner or support group, let's be honest, we're silently taking on too much and we know it, right?

Oprah said, "You can have it all. Just not all at once." Now I'm not gonna go against the Great Lady O ... but I disagree. I think we can have it all at once—we just can't do it all ourselves.

The game has changed. We can live our best lives like never before; we just can't do it as one single human being. We need a village of help and support.

According to Xuan Zhao, researcher and social psychologist from Stanford University, people actually want to help more often than we give them credit for. Zhao's research admits that people can find it difficult to ask for help, but she says it's because we often underestimate how happy helping makes people feel.[3]

Stanford psychologist Professor Dale Miller's research suggests that we hesitate to ask for help because when thinking about people's motivation to help us, we often apply a more pessimistic mindset and are alert to any areas of self-interest. He reasons that Western cultures are more inclined to value independence and asking others to go out of their way to help can feel like the wrong thing to do, or the selfish thing to do.[4]

Both experts highlight the fact that the opposite of what we generally think is more true: we are naturally prosocial, and most of us actually want to make a positive difference in the lives of others.

So, not asking for help isn't just a problem for people with a penchant for martyrdom or with low self-worth; it's as common as a house fly and even more annoying. Why? Because most people *want* to help. And for mentors and coaches, it's their life's purpose. It's what they are gifted at doing. It's what they love to do. It's what they have been trained to do.

If you can't ask for help, then I can guarantee the problem arises from you. The mentor wants to help and lead you. Here, I can speak for myself. Helping and mentoring others is my soul contract and mission. It is my purpose here on Earth, and it is derived from being great at what I do.

### ∾ "I can't afford a coach or mentor."

This is one of the most common barriers, and it's a fair call. Everyone has different financial circumstances for different reasons. Even though I am financially free now, it wasn't always the case. I had many years of struggle, working my ass off to make ends meet. Dane and I have had many moments where we just stared at each other, shaking our heads and wondering what the hell we were gonna do.

We've scrimped and saved and tried to juggle the sums to pay bills, and sometimes, no matter how hard we tried, we were always having to work harder and longer just to stay afloat. So, when people say "I can't afford a mentor or coach," I get it! I've been there myself many times.

I often suggest to people to start where they can. Start with books, audios, and podcasts. Libraries are open, and now we have free access to so much amazing material. YouTube is jam-packed with self-development content.

If life is really tough for you right now, it doesn't mean you can't be coached. There are a lot of free and low budget workshops, events and self-paced spaces that you can attend online or in person.

 Scan the QR code to learn more about the life-changing work NMCM (Nadine Muller Coaching and Mentoring) leads thousands through.

For me, the greatest investment I made was hiring a high-end coach. At the time, it was a major stretch for me financially, but it paid back tenfold. My career skyrocketed, and my ability to impact more people increased. My sphere of influence became greater, and I felt aligned with my greatest destiny.

For those who are ready, hiring an incredible mentor is not an investment in them as such; it's an investment in *you*. It's an investment in RISING.

Rising means getting into the ring. You can't rise as a spectator. You gotta go in boots and all.

## ∞ "I can't trust them. I've had a bad experience in the past."

This is a biggie. Some people have been burnt by ordinary coaches and mentors that have betrayed trust or stolen their well-earned money. It's fair enough to be discerning. In fact, you should be discerning! I encourage it.

There are a lot of coaches and mentors who are good at marketing themselves but maybe aren't so great at the thing they're marketing. I encourage people to be like an investigator—research the fuck out of the person you're trusting! This isn't a Tinder booty call; this is your freakin' life. It's important.

Follow prospective coaches on social media and ask people who have used them before. Yes, you must do your due diligence before jumping in boots and all.

One of my gorgeous clients Belle was one of the trusting souls who had just come off the back of a bad coaching experience.

She had paid big bucks for six group coaching sessions and a one-to-one session as part of her package. She was so pumped to do the one-to-one … but when she reached out to get it, the coach was always busy and brushing her off. She had forked out good money for a private session, but the coach never came good on his offer. His whole sales pitch promised results and a personal "exclusive" coaching call with him, but it never happened. He would razzle and dazzle the group during the group calls, pouring his charisma all over the place, but he never delivered on the one-to-one. Sure, he was a super busy in-demand guy, BUT he was incongruent. He was a captivating sales smoothy, and he made promises he didn't keep.

When I quizzed Belle as to what research she did, she admitted she did very little. She saw a social media video and got instantly excited to join his exclusive coaching group. Plus, there were apparently three spots left, so she felt she had to act fast—and she did. She pulled out her Visa card and signed up to his coaching package, which sounded absolutely fabulous, right then and there. One of her main reasons for signing up was the one-to-one session offer. She wanted that one-to-one session so bad, but she never got it. No wonder she felt burnt.

Now, we have all been there. We have all experienced buyer's remorse at some point. But this ain't a pair of heels you can return—this is your life.

There are thieves in all industries, but you must take responsibility for the part you played in the transaction. Did you not listen to your intuition? Did you not ask a single question because you were too afraid they'd think badly of you? Did you not do your research?

I want my clients to be discerning with who they trust. Hire people who have a good track record, deliver what they promise, and don't charge you your annual salary while giving peanuts in return. When you've been burnt, it doesn't mean you never try again. It means you have more experience and won't let the same thing happen again.

I recommend sharing your feedback and experience with your coach. Let them know you were burnt and felt wounded (yes, it's a fucking wound). Communicate your concerns about getting hurt again. Or getting shafted financially. A good coach will empathize and make it their duty to maintain your trust. You should never go against your intuition. If a coach is saying all the right things but you don't feel the words are congruent with their actions, address it straight away.

You see, this really is about *you*. It's about your power, your ability to take a stand. As the old adage says, "If you don't know what you stand for, you will fall for anything."

This doesn't eliminate the fact that there will be shitty and incongruent coaches and mentors out there. We see this in every industry, job, and role, right? They will always exist, but you don't have to hire them. Do your research. Trust your gut. Find the coach who's right for you.

## ∾ "What can they give me that I can't get from myself?"

Because I was so anti-help, I nearly lost the opportunity to grow exponentially. I still believe in the mantra, "If it's meant to be, it's up to me." I preach that like an evangelist, and I live my life by it.

Unapologetic radical responsibility is my jam; if I could be a poster girl for it, I would. But this doesn't mean you can get *everything* you need from yourself. We are social humans, and we thrive on connection and community. Our entire survival is based on us helping one another. We wouldn't have survived without the deep bonds between us.

Many strong independent women sometimes feel that getting help is a backward step. We, as women, have battled so hard to gain and retain our sense of sovereignty and independence that we are reluctant to be in a situation that we believe suppresses our control.

But here's the thing ... you should never give up your authority! A coach is not a tyrant; they are more like a cheerleader, a supporter. If you've ever seen a Rocky movie, it's still Rocky who goes into the fight swinging punches, but it's his coach yelling out, "Use the uppercut," or "Watch his right hook." It's Rocky who does the work and claims the victory and bruises, but his coach can see things that he can't. Why? Because Rocky is in the ring, and his coach is on the outside. His coach can see things from his vantage point that Rocky can't. His coach isn't about to cop a punch to the face, so he can sit back without the survival burst of adrenaline and cortisol clouding his thoughts and see what Rocky can't.

I've had many people claim they really don't need a coach or mentor because they are already neck-deep in their own personal development. I know what happens ... they feel already involved because they scroll Insta, jump on live events, engage in conscious conversations, and consume meaningful podcasts and YouTube content. I love this stuff too; I'm such an advocate for good meaningful content, but I also got stuck in the same mindset. I really thought I was *doing* my development. And I was ... but it was based on what I *liked*, NOT what I *needed*.

It is easy to scroll and listen and watch things you're interested in, BUT the algorithms are set up to give you more of what you watch. You can learn and learn and learn and be full of amazing knowledge, but you can still overlook the shadows that control your beliefs and behaviors. Because, just like a dog can't smell its own scent, we can't see our own blind spots!

So you could be dedicated to your growth and still overlook the most vital ingredient for a breakthrough.

I realized that my dedication to learning was insatiable. I loved it so much (and still do) that I was consuming educational content faster than you could say "addict." But after a while, I realized that my energy wasn't focused; it was going in many different, albeit amazing, directions, and I was shooting blanks all over the place. I was listening to amazing audios, reading the most incredible books, and taking shitloads of brilliant workshops and courses, BUT there was something missing.

Other leaders in my industry experienced rapid growth, like mind-blowing type of growth, the type that made me take notice, but I didn't. The common denominator? They were working with coaches or mentors who were setting them up to win.

Let me share a little story …

One day, an old gold miner retired. He was too old to dig and had already made his fortune finding gold. He decided to teach others all he knew so he could help them achieve success without all the struggle he went through. After all, finding gold wasn't an easy thing to do.

His first two students were eager to learn and enthusiastic about making their fortune. The old man took them to a piece of land and told them, "There is gold here!" The first man was so excited that he grabbed his shovel and ran off. He was determined to find the gold first and make his fortune. He started digging lots of holes.

The second man watched him, and then turned to the old man and asked, "Do you know where it is?"

The old man smiled at him and whispered, "It's toward the north, down deeper than you'd think."

The first man had dug hundreds of small holes all over the place. It looked like he was digging the most and was going to find the gold. The second man dug one hole, methodically, dirt pile by dirt pile, deeper than he would normally go. The first man was exhausted from his epic effort. The second man stayed laser-focused and kept digging, although also tired from his work.

The old man walked off home. He knew what would happen. He knew the outcome before it unfolded. Why? Because he had spent his entire life gold mining. He knew where the gold was. He took them straight to it. But one listened, asked questions, and honored his wisdom, while the other was so eager that he overlooked the most essential ingredient for success—learning from a master.

So, what can you get from a coach or mentor that you can't get yourself? Mmm … where do I begin?

- Wisdom
- Hard-earned experience
- Guidance
- Seeing red flags and opportunities you can't
- Objectiveness
- Radical honesty from observation
- Perspective
- Knowing where the gold is!

## The Gold You Are Looking For

Finding someone with deep experience who has wildly succeeded and is willing to share their knowledge and wisdom with you is essentially like striking gold. It's a eureka moment.

I know that sounds extreme—but it's not. It's the slipstream to success. If you've ever ridden a bike behind someone, you will know that if you slip behind the leader you can enjoy an easier ride. They take the headwind, and you can pedal less. It's like a beautiful vortex of minimized effort, but you don't lose direction.

When you see a flock of geese flying in the V formation, they are flying smart, conserving their energy for the long migratory flight and using the slipstream of the bird in front. They all arrive at the same time while using the slipstream method to their best advantage.

Our dreams can be like a long road or flight, and instead of exhausting ourselves and pedaling hard uphill alone, we can simply slide in behind an amazing leader and gain the advantages of a premade slipstream.

I guess it's kind of like the people who make the first path in rugged terrain—they cut down trees and bushes and hack their way through dense scrub to make a path that others can walk.

A good coach or mentor can collapse time! They can literally save you years of hard work, lost income, and misdirected effort. This is called a quantum leap (also my zone of genius!), easily one of my favorite things I love seeing my clients experience!

## Finding a Good Coach or Mentor

I know, finding a good reputable expert with proven results that you actually click with is a big ask. But believe me, they really do exist. You're not looking for a mythical unicorn. Good coaches and mentors are out there, waiting to help. Sure, you must discern the good from the bad, but you are equipped with your own magical compass of intuition that will help you find the right person for you.

When I hire mentors, I play big (I'll never NOT have them!). They are an asset to me personally as a company director and for my empire expansion. The return on investment speaks volumes to me. They know I am here and ready to play a big game, and I ain't hiring a coach who hasn't won a Super Bowl.

## Differences between a Coach and Mentor

Now, a lot of people don't know there's a difference between coaches and mentors. They do cross over to some degree, but there are distinct differences. A coach is much more directive and performance-driven for a specific amount of time, whereas a mentor is more focused on long-term development and guidance. So sometimes people are looking for a coach when they really want a mentor, and vice versa.

I'm all about results and empowerment. My style is about ensuring the person I'm working with expresses their highest potential. I adapt my style to meet what the client needs. Some people need to be challenged; others need to be nurtured with gentleness. A great coach should be able to adapt their style to suit the needs of the client.

| COACH | MENTOR |
|---|---|
| Set duration | Ongoing relationship |
| Task oriented | Relationship oriented |
| Open | Confidential |
| Short term | Long term |
| Formal relationship | Informal relationship |
| Performance driven | Development driven |
| Focused on achieving goals | Focused on support and guidance |
| Focused on specific development areas | Focused on professional and personal success |
| Focused on instructing | Focused on listening |
| Behavioral transformation | Personal transformation |
| Coach may drive it, but mentee must want to learn | Mentee drives it |

## The People Who Level Up—Quantum Leap

Now, I have seen some wild and audacious transformations during my time as a coach and mentor. Mind-boggling changes that are seriously off the charts. For example, one couple were on the brink of divorce, and they decided to spend $6,000 on our couple's retreat. It was their last go at saving their marriage. They had tried multiple counselors and avenues and were on the merry-go-round of support, yet they couldn't break their well-grooved toxic patterns.

The night before, they had a fight about the amount of money they'd spent on the retreat. The wife shared the details of the fight with the group at the retreat, explaining that her husband was complaining about the huge sum of money.

My husband Dane asked him, "How costly do you think a divorce would be?"

The man looked shocked, then cracked a smile. "That's true," he said.

"Is saving your marriage worth the investment?" Dane asked.

The man looked at his wife. "Every cent, and more," he said.

The wife smiled, and they began to explore other ways they could invest in each other—emotionally, mentally, spiritually. They began to explore what their attitudes and scorekeeping ways were costing them emotionally, mentally, financially, and spiritually.

In a nutshell, this couple leveled up. They took an entirely new approach to their marriage. They saw it differently; they acted differently; they spoke differently. They took a wild quantum leap into new territory to save their marriage. They knew that the price of not changing would be crippling.

Why do some people experience such amazing results? They shift their entire frequency and operate on a whole new level. They change their minds about things and commit to becoming the best version of themselves. Now that may sound cliché, but it's true.

## The Leap

Quantum leap basically means a "huge and often sudden increase or advance."

In my experience, we can all experience quantum leaps in our lives. Scientists have even researched these extraordinary happenings and studied it at the quantum level with subatomic particles and quantum waves. Now, I'm not the person to offer a physics lesson, but it seems that a group of psychologists have also experienced this phenomenon and now even have a new interdisciplinary field called "quantum psychology" that investigates psychological phenomena within the field of quantum mechanics. Wild!

Quantum leaps work on a subatomic level, and they happen when people make incredible paradigm shifts in the way they think, behave, and perceive. Quantum leapers are upgrading their minds, bodies, and lives to new levels, and they are moving and actioning to match it while most others are still "thinking about it."

Physicist and author of *Quantum Jumps* Cynthia Sue Larson is an expert on quantum reality and suggests that we indeed make these leaps. She says:

Quantum jumps require both a flash of insight that a new reality is possible, and a burst of sufficient energy to make the leap. Those decisive instants when we feel simultaneously energized by knowledge of a better reality and inspired to act are the moments that we make quantum jumps.[5]

Being fueled by new insights and radical shifts in thinking

opens the door to taking quantum leaps. Having a vision and marinating yourself in inspiration, faith, action, and accountability create the space for epic things to occur.

So what are the characteristics of a typical quantum leaper?

## They Operate at a New Frequency and Have Agency

I have noticed that people who transform their lives have transformed their minds and emotions. They upgrade their beliefs and aren't afraid to let go of outdated beliefs and behaviors.

They participate in their dreams and are willing to be challenged if required. In short, these people are **coachable**. They are ready and ripe for growth.

Scientists and psychologists are now studying "transformative experiences," which they call TEs. They are also studying the growth that can occur after traumatic experiences, called post traumatic growth (PTG). Although the characteristics and signatures of such occurrences are still being debated, one thing is for sure: they happen more frequently than first predicted.

I believe that transformation occurs more often in those willing to reinvent their minds and beliefs. Of course, there are exceptional circumstances, such as when someone receives instant insight—*satori*—or revelation into their issues. But for many, it can mean changing habits, changing friends, changing environments, changing their minds. Or as stated by Swiss psychologist and genetic epistemologist Jean Piaget, "We organize our worlds by first organizing ourselves."[6]

According to researcher and expert in constructive psychology, Michael Mahoney ...

Rapid personality transformations do occur ... [such change] involves enduring shifts in people's sense of themselves and their perceptions of the world. The phenomenon of quantum change or rapid transformation deserves our continuing theoretical and research attention. It appears to be more common than psychologists had assumed.[7]

Mahoney's research also illuminates the fact that the act of continuing to evolve, grow, and experience the full capacity of life involves "active agency."[8] Essentially, we must continuously act in our own lives, and this means growing, changing, and adapting.

Those who change, thrive.

## They Don't Ask the Opinions of the Wrong People

As you've heard, I'm a massive fan of asking the *right* people for advice, those who have succeeded in the very same thing you desire to succeed in. If you want to be the world's best parent, would you ask someone who has never had children how to best raise them? Or if you want a second opinion on your Pap smear results, are you going to ask your dentist? That would be insane, not to mention awkward.

Yet it never ceases to amaze me how many people fail at this 101 lesson. I know you may have an awesome family and some amazing friends—and if they understand your business or dreams, then by all means ask them for advice—but I have seen so many talented people never start things or start to doubt their abilities because they ran it past their parents, high school friends, or grandparents. If your BFF is working as an employee in a 9–5 job and you ask them for advice about your entrepreneurial journey, then I'm not sure their advice (even if well-intentioned) will be valid.

I love my mom; I respect my mom; I value her input, but I don't ask her what to do in my business. Why would I? She has never run a business. I ask Mom about things I know she is experienced in, like raising good humans, evolving my compassion, cultural traditions I can pass down to my kids, and the wisdom she has gained from her own life.

When people experience rapid growth, it's because they're calibrating to a frequency outside their own. They are conferring with those in the know and not relying on those who simply want to flex their opinion.

Let's be honest—every social media keyboard warrior has an opinion! Opinions *are* important … just make sure you listen to the right ones. Someone sitting at home unemployed, munching on pretzels and binge-watching *Desperate Housewives* while they throw opinions at you about how to better your business, isn't worth listening to. One of my valued clients telling me how I could improve my business, or highlighting issues I may not have seen—yep, that *is* worth listening to.

Once again, use discernment. You're not here to please every human that crosses your path; you're here to live wildly alive as YOU! In doing so, you will impact others through who you are.

## They Surround Themselves with Like-Minded People and Leaders

When I started growing my business, I began sitting at some tables that I thought were waayyyy beyond my comfort zone. Tables with brilliant people doing brilliant things. I listened to and hired some high-caliber people. I watched; I listened; I learned; I applied myself.

I hung out with big movers and shakers, high-frequency people doing amazing things with their lives and businesses. I unapologetically tapped into the way they thought, the way they saw possibility, abundance, working, and life.

It becomes like a magical virus that you want to be infected with—the incredible buzz of brilliance, creativity, and possibility coursing through your veins. I began to see what was possible for my life. I began to visualize how good it could get! I began to feel energized and focused like never before. I had active agency in my planning.

Surrounding myself with like-minded people and leaders was a game changer. Hiring them to be my coaches and mentors was life-changing.

As Sir Isaac Newton said, "If I have seen further it is by standing on the shoulders of Giants."

## They Commit to Their Growth

The people who revolutionize their lives are committed to their own growth. They have active agency and aren't fixated on being an overnight success. They want to stay the course and bring their highest good into the world.

Having a growth mindset has been studied extensively, and time and time again it reveals that having a commitment to growth and believing in your ability to learn is fundamental to success in any capacity, personal and professional. The term "growth mindset," which is the belief that one has the capacity to grow, was coined by Carol Dweck, who studied the fact that those who believed they could develop their skills had better long-term outcomes than those who saw their skills and talents as "fixed."

> *"You don't know what your abilities are until you make a full commitment to developing them."*
> **—CAROL S. DWECK**

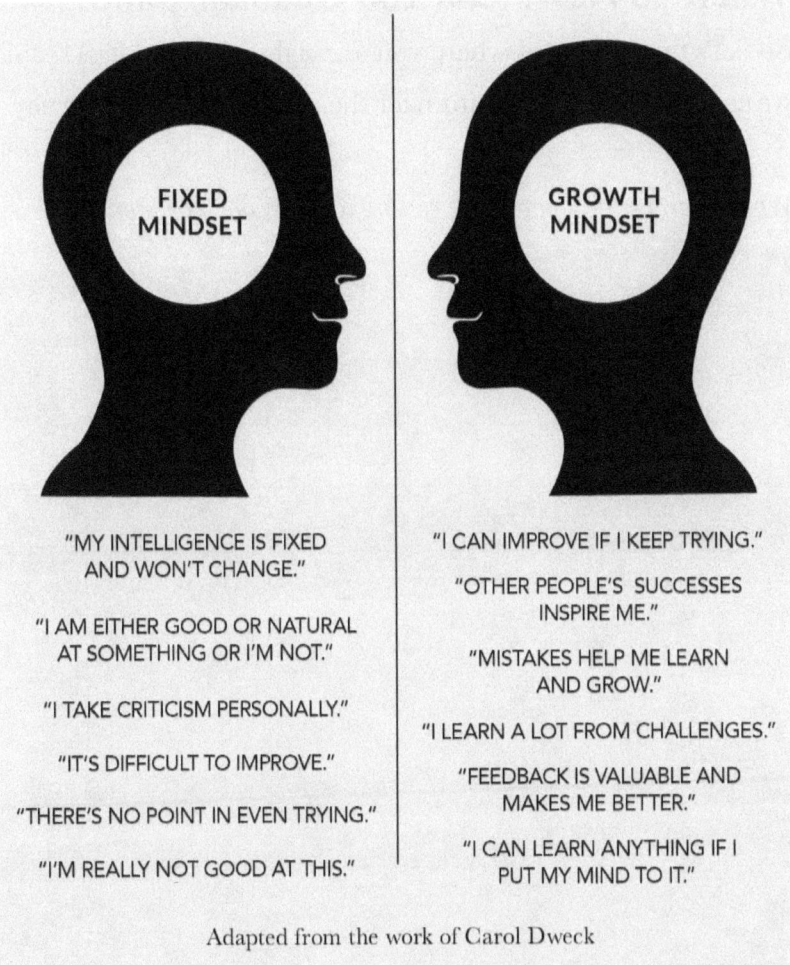

Adapted from the work of Carol Dweck

Research shows that those who commit to their growth experience better outcomes and increased wellbeing and happiness. Those who are willing to learn new things, or new ways of thinking and being, adapt better than those who remain in a fixed mindset.

## Where to Now? Can You Quantum Jump?

So, let's take a look at where you are right now, and let's see if we can gain some momentum for the next step in your journey.

*What is preventing you from getting a good coach or mentor?*

*What's that costing you, emotionally, mentally, spiritually, physically (time, money, effort)?*

.....................................................................................................................................
.....................................................................................................................................
.....................................................................................................................................
.....................................................................................................................................
.....................................................................................................................................
.....................................................................................................................................
.....................................................................................................................................
.....................................................................................................................................
.....................................................................................................................................
.....................................................................................................................................
.....................................................................................................................................
.....................................................................................................................................
.....................................................................................................................................
.....................................................................................................................................
.....................................................................................................................................

*What's the one main area of focus where you want radical results?*

.....................................................................................................................................
.....................................................................................................................................
.....................................................................................................................................

*Make a list of people you know achieving the results you desire.*

................................................................................

................................................................................

................................................................................

................................................................................

................................................................................

................................................................................

................................................................................

................................................................................

*What's one step you could take today in the direction you want to go?*

................................................................................

................................................................................

................................................................................

Scan the QR code for RISE to greatness resources, experiences, and exclusive content for your journey of growth.

## CHAPTER 5

# COURAGE IS YOUR COMPASS

Courage isn't all swords and battle and warrior cries. It's often a quiet strength that lingers in your heart and stays true to your values and personal integrity. Following your inner compass naturally cultivates courage.

No matter where you're heading, you are going to need to build your muscles of courage. In my opinion, courage is an inside job ... it is often unseen by others who don't know the internal battles we face.

The well-known quote, "Be kind, for everyone you meet is fighting a hard battle," is true. You just never know the warfare that people are facing inside. It could be a battle of mental or physical health, a battle to gain confidence and self-esteem, a battle to be seen and heard, a battle to be loved and accepted.

A battle to survive the shitstorm of grief and heartache that life has provided.

For some, it takes courage to show affection and speak the words they feel. For others, it could take courage to face a financial crisis or relationship crossroads. Courage comes in many forms, and it takes courage to face our fears as well as chase our dreams. As author and artist Mary Anne Radmacher said, "Courage doesn't always roar. Sometimes courage is the little voice at the end of the day that says I'll try again tomorrow."

Yes, courage can be loud and proud and roaring with activist energy, and it can be soft, quiet, gentle, and very subtle. It can simply be trying again the next day.

I believe it is the acts of bravery that take place within ourselves that reflect our true courage. Acts such as looking at our beliefs, challenging our outdated patterns and behaviors, seeking more from our gifts and talents, offering ourselves up for service. Facing our demons and shining our light.

Sometimes courage can be simply saying:
*I love you.*
*Please help me.*
*I need support.*
*Do you need help?*
*I feel uncomfortable.*
*I would like you to be my coach/mentor.*
*I'm sorry for hurting you.*
*Please forgive me.*

*I will try again tomorrow.*

Sometimes courage can be:
*Asking an old friend for coffee.*
*Forgiving someone who hurt you.*
*Making the first move.*
*Asking for a raise.*
*Giving up an old habit.*
*Saying sorry.*
*Trying something new.*

## Courage Is Not the Absence of Fear

Nelson Mandela is loved all around the world for his tremendous bravery ... yet he said, "I learned that courage was not the absence of fear, but the triumph over it. The brave man is not he who does not feel afraid, but he who conquers that fear."

We aren't supposed to rid ourselves of fear or be so tough that we don't feel it. We are human, and the fear reflex is installed in our nervous systems for damn good reasons, like running away from danger or fighting for survival. But in our modern era, we are often "on," and our bodies are receiving an overload of information, images, fearmongering headlines, and more. We are in a society that feeds our nervous systems a lot of fear, and our bodies are whipped into an anxious and adrenaline-filled state more than they are wired to be. Being in a state of chronic stress and fear is not what we were designed for.

We must remember that we are naturally courageous beings.

We are wisely courageous, and we have survived for thousands of years because of our genius ability to adapt, innovate, and survive.

A child is born naturally courageous. They seek to walk and talk and fall down and get back up again. They seek to explore and try new foods and new adventures, yet they don't need to manufacture or conjure up courage. They naturally have it because they are curious and aren't worried about what others think about them.

Children are natural seekers, and the act of seeking shows us new horizons. It's a courageous act to seek new horizons for yourself, to step out of your comfort zone, cultural bonds, or country of birth to see new things. It's a courageous act to defy any dysfunctional conditioning of your upbringing in order to discover new ways of being and living.

We aren't supposed to be without fear, but we are equipped with the discernment to know when to listen to it and when not to.

## Are You Using Fear, or Letting Fear Use You?

Fear is designed to activate your nervous system to keep you safe during times of crisis. For example, you hear a tree cracking and falling; you look up, and your fight-or-flight response kicks in and swamps your body with adrenaline so you can quickly dodge the danger. Kinda helpful, right?

The issue with igniting the fear response too often is that it whips the body into a state of chronic stress and makes us more prone to anxiety, illness, exhaustion, and depression. We aren't designed to be in a perpetual state of fight or flight. It depletes our mind, body, and spirit. And yet, we have got so accustomed to living with stress that we don't know what it feels like to be without it. To be free from it. To let it come and go only appropriately. Our fight-or-flight response is designed wisely. It's supposed to be used when we are in imminent danger or need to act swiftly; it's not designed to be triggered all day long.

We have five basic human responses to fear: flight, fight, freeze, fawn, or flop.

The problem with our modern-day society is that it is constantly triggering our stress response—bad news on social media and TV, anxiety about work deadlines, and the constant stress to perform in all areas of life. It's abnormal. Thus, we get abnormal responses to an abnormal environment. We never allow our nervous systems to go into their natural state of rest and rejuvenation. It's a vicious cycle. We feel bombarded by negativity or stress (or both!).

You see, we have allowed stress to use us, rather than us using it. We can have optimal stress that keeps us alert, productive, and engaged, and we can have burnout and exhaustion.

If you want to RISE above the masses who are controlled daily by fear and stress, then you must learn how to use stress rather than let it use you. You must become the master of your own mind and emotions, and therefore master of your own internal environment and destiny. Too much stress is dangerous and unhelpful, but the right amount of healthy stress can help you feel engaged with life and super productive.

> *"Calm mind brings inner strength and self-confidence, so that's very important for good health."*
> —DALAI LAMA

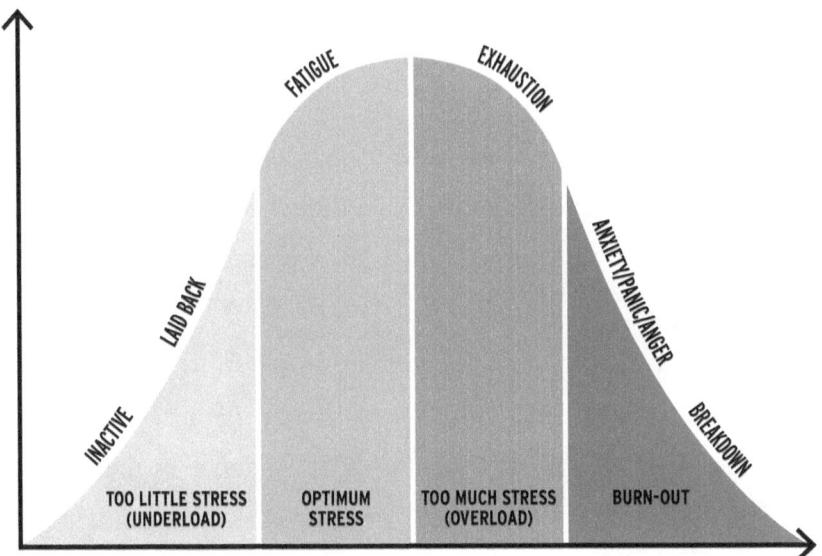

Courage is not the total absence of fear. It is, as Nelson Mandela said, "the triumph over it," and that is an inner game. The first place we can test our courage is in our thinking.

Thinking courageous instead of victim-based thoughts is a good start. Unsubscribing from influencers and social media posts which disempower you. Educating yourself about fear and anxiety and the way it impacts the nervous system. Learning about the sympathetic and parasympathetic systems in our bodies. Making meditation and relaxation a part of your routine.

Research professor and expert on vulnerability, shame, and courage, Dr. Brené Brown uses the mantra, "Courage over comfort" and says, "You can choose courage, or you can choose comfort, but you cannot choose both."

I believe that is true. Choosing courage may be risky; it may be challenging, but it certainly is worth it.

## Bravery vs. Courage

Bravery and courage are in fact different, although many people think they're the same.

The origin of the word bravery stems from the medieval Latin *bravus*, meaning "cutthroat, villain" and developed into the Italian *bravo* "brave, bold," which originally stemmed from "wild, savage."[1]

Bravery is the act of being daring or bold in the face of danger. It often is associated with a lack of fear. A "just do it now" attitude. A full-on burst of power and confidence in the face of danger. Many epic movies show our heroes as brave soldiers.

Courage is different though. The origin of the word "courage" comes from the Latin term *cor*, which means "heart." *"Coeur"* is also the French word for "heart." To have courage means to "have heart." Circa 1300, the term *corage* was considered to mean "heart (as the seat of emotions)."[2]

Courage is more of a conscious choice, an act of virtue that draws something out of you. Courage is required to face a difficult or dangerous situation, but it does not negate the feelings of fear or concern. Courage may act in the face of them, but it does not dismiss or not feel them. Courage is expressed with an awareness that one is acting despite fear. Often, courageous people have a set of values or principles that they believe in and hold true to.

Gandhi was a man of courage. His small and frail frame did not make him a physically dominant figure, in fact, quite the opposite. But his values, spiritual principles, and conviction in nonviolent opposition gave him the courage to defy injustice and stand firm in his beliefs. His moral and spiritual courage were so strong and clear that his virtuous acts created a movement. His courage was aligned with his heart values, making him one of the most powerful figures in history.

> *"To embark on the journey towards*
> *your goals and dreams requires bravery.*
> *To remain on that path requires courage."*
> —STEVE MARABOLI

## The Six Types of Courage

I believe it takes courage to RISE and live a life that is true to you. We are all unique and individual, and that means we have personal differences and personality differences. Human beings all sitting around in a circle, holding hands, and singing *kumbaya* together is a world I'd like to be a part of, but it's a fantasy world that doesn't yet exist. For some reason, we haven't collectively raised our consciousness high enough to end all war, social injustice, and disparity. We still have shitloads of work to do! And in order to do it, we must act despite fear. We must create the world we want to live in.

We must begin with ourselves!

To act in accordance with your soul takes courage. But the good news is, the more you work your courage muscles, the stronger they become, and the stronger you become. The stronger we become individually, the stronger we become collectively. Now, of course, I don't mean strength in merely the physical sense; I mean the more united we become, the more compassionate, the more capable, the more empowered we become.

I have spent a HUGE amount of time exercising my courage muscles. I have faced and battled so many inner demons that I now thrive in slaying them. I want the same for you. And I promise you with all my heart that once you slay some demons of doubt and fear, you grow stronger. You reignite your heroic journey, and you start to believe in yourself more and more.

That is why courage is vital to your journey. That's why Eleanor Roosevelt said, "You must do the thing you think you cannot do."

For if we RISE above our self-imposed limitations, we shatter the illusions that are holding us back. We form a new identity, a new belief about what is possible for us. We build a new bridge to walk over that takes us to a new world of our own making.

We simply must defy the voice that tells us that we are too small, too weak, too dumb, too smart, too busy, too unskilled, too introverted, too whatever, and we must overcome the invisible wall that is holding us back from our full potential.

We must RISE higher than our conditioned minds and slay the demons that lurk in the shadows of doubt, despair, and victimhood. You are a warrior of the light, not a servant of doubt.

*"Dig deeper within the confines of your inner warrior. I guarantee, you haven't yet seen the real you, who is ridiculously fearless and outrageously unstoppable."*
—HIRAL NAGDA

The six types of courage I would like to explore are:
- Physical courage
- Social courage
- Moral courage
- Emotional courage
- Intellectual courage
- Spiritual courage

Let's do a deep dive into each one.

## ∽ Physical Courage ∽

This is the courage most people watch at the movies and think sums up "courage." *Gladiator, Braveheart,* and *Superman* all show epic feats of physical strength and mastery. Now, physical courage is certainly admirable, and we love to watch superhuman moments in sport and marvel at the extraordinary precision and power of elite athletes. But often physical courage comes with mental and emotional courage too. The boxer who steps into the ring isn't merely a physical warrior, but a mental and emotional one too. The boxer faces the possibility of being hurt, losing the fight, and feeling disappointment or even humiliation. Physical courage can mean to continue with something despite the fear of physical harm, for example, rescuing someone from a fire, protecting someone from a potential threat, shielding your loved ones from a storm. These huge acts of courage often make the news, and many people get rewarded with bravery medals.

Physical courage is something we are mesmerized by in our society. But these acts can also happen on a smaller scale (without the news headlines). For example, a client of mine wanted to complete a marathon despite having never been a runner and having a slight disability. Her act of courage was a huge turning point for her. She trained and trained and completed the marathon. Although she was blistered and sore and didn't get the time she wanted—she finished! She completed what she set out to do, and that courageous act changed the way she saw herself.

When I was a personal trainer and coaching health and fitness online, I was often shocked at how many people didn't even attempt to find out how many push-ups they could do, or how many sit-ups they could do in a specified time frame. They were too scared of the physical pain (even if it was only a minute). But it wasn't the pain they were really scared of ... They were afraid to embarrass themselves, afraid to know their limits or discover their edge and be disappointed in what they learned. They were afraid of humiliation and the self-discovery of not being good enough. But the sad reality is, the ones who never tried never succeeded. The ones who tried always got better. Even the clients who only managed a handful of sit-ups in a minute, but still tried, always ended up improving beyond their expectations. Why? Because they had the courage to try.

Having physical courage doesn't have to mean marathons and fierce battles. It could be simply going for a daily walk, doing a type of fitness class you've never done before, joining a running group, having a physical strength goal like doing five chin-ups, or trying Pilates for the first time.

> *"Fear is a reaction. Courage is a decision."*
> —WINSTON CHURCHILL

## ~ Social Courage ~

Social courage is the courage to put yourself in social situations where you may feel vulnerable. We have all had to build our social courage muscles from the time we were young, and no one is immune to a so-called "failure" or two. Social courage often involves risk—the risk of feeling embarrassed, feeling excluded, or being judged or ridiculed.

Social courage should be taught to us when we are young, rather than getting "discovered" by us through the life of hard knocks. A traumatic social experience in childhood or young adulthood can leave us feeling socially wounded and scarred. For many, that can create an awkwardness and a dysfunction in relationships. Some people become extremely introverted or avoidant in social settings as a way to cope with the perceived threat those settings present.

It can take incredible acts of social courage to make friends, to network with work colleagues, to find a date, to give a speech, to accept a trophy or reward, to present a new idea to your boss.

From the time we are born to the time we die, we are confronted with an array of social settings to navigate, and doing this takes courage. It takes courage to put yourself "out there" and learn the rules of social engagement. Of course, each setting is different, and each one comes with its own set of rules. For example, socializing at a work conference may be super uncomfortable for you, yet you may feel comfortable leading a small group discussion with the same colleagues. Or you may detest going to your in-laws' house for Christmas, with the extra relatives, but feel absolutely happy to have them over for dinner at your house.

Social events and environments are very unique to the individual, and we can feel comfortable with some people and situations and not others. The hard part is getting out of our social comfort zones! And doing that takes courage.

For example, I invested what would be considered a ridiculous amount of money to attend a leadership convention with some incredibly successful, smart, and influential people and leaders. I paid a massive amount to "pick their brains" and learn what they had done (or had not done) to grow their businesses. At first, I felt nerves and heard that inner mean girl voice trying to creep in ... They all seemed to know one another and were very comfortable in that setting. I was the newbie and felt socially awkward. My brain started to say crazy things like, *These people are wayyy more "successful" than you, Nadine, what are you doing here?*

I had a quick bout of impostor syndrome and had to quickly rectify my conscious brain, in its attempt to derail me, and the spiraling belief of not belonging. It wasn't easy though. I was in an unfamiliar space with highly influential people who were far more successful than I was at the time. My mind was yelling at me to run back to my safe place, with my safe people, and do my safe things. But here's the thing: these people were doing the very thing I wanted to do, and I needed to learn from them. I wanted to learn from them. I wanted to discover the things they knew that I didn't. So … I had to change me. I had to muster some social courage and step into foreign territory. Even if they were discussing terms and results I hadn't normalized—YET. Even if they seemed cliquey and comfortable with each other. I decided to ask some questions of the woman sitting next to me. I asked her about herself (a safe place where people have almost zero resistance to communicating with you), and I slowly built my social confidence through the avenue of social courage.

Now, some people say, "Well, that's easy for you, Nadine. You are used to talking to lots of people and presenting in front of groups."

And I remind them, "That's what you see now. I had to build that muscle and develop it too. I wasn't born presenting and guest speaking and leading workshops and retreats … I had to learn that skill, and many of the skills I learned in business required me to put myself into uncomfortable situations with new people, which took a large dose of social courage."

*"Enthusiasm is a form of social courage."*
—GRETCHEN RUBIN

## Moral Courage

Moral courage involves our values, ethics, morals, and integrity. It often means doing what you believe is right regardless of opposition or the risk of earning disapproval. Moral courage involves standing up for your convictions despite resistance.

Many great leaders have moral courage. When Rosa Parks said "no" to giving up her seat on the bus to a white passenger, her moral courage fueled change. Others in agreement with her individual moral courage became a movement of global change. Women suffragettes protesting and demanding that women have a voice and be allowed to vote was another example of moral courage. They faced huge opposition for their plight but changed the world for the better.

Moral courage can often cause conflict and disrupt the mainstream views or cultural and social views of the time. Someone choosing to act on their personal and moral views rather than the political or socially embedded views of others requires moral courage.

In a world of many cultures and creeds, moral courage can be misunderstood and may seem conflicting. For example, a Christian may protest the act of abortion based on a belief formed by their values and morals, while a feminist may protest for proabortion based on a different belief formed by their values and morals. They both believe their "truth" and are acting in accordance with it.

While we may not always have the same morals and beliefs, acting on behalf of what is "right" in terms of basic human rights is a simple principle we can all adhere to. Human rights are those we have simply because we exist as human beings—they are not granted by any political party or state. The Universal Declaration of Human Rights (UDHR) says, "These universal rights are inherent to us all, regardless of nationality, sex, national or ethnic origin, color, religion, language, or any other status. They range from the most fundamental - the right to life - to those that make life worth living, such as the rights to food, education, work, health, and liberty."[3]

So why am I banging on about this? Because we often forget our sovereignty. We forget that we are powerful beings with basic human rights. We forget that simply by existing we have an inheritance of rights that can be exercised and leaned on. You deserve to know that moral courage can be exercised through your human right to work, eat, be educated, and live a healthy, free, and happy life.

When Malala Yousafzai was shot in the face by the Taliban on her way home from school in Pakistan for voicing her belief in women's education, her moral courage became the cornerstone for a girl's right to education. Her moral courage was imbued with a deep altruism for her fellow schoolmates and all young women in oppressed societies. She simply knew that her worth as a human being and as a female meant she deserved an education. She had the right to live free and be educated, and she exercised those rights.

Many authors, investigative journalists, whistleblowers, human rights activists, political leaders, and scientists have been the beacons of change in the world through their stances and moral courage.

I believe that knowing our rights is one thing, and exercising them is another. As professor and bestselling author Dr. Margaret Heffernan reminds us, "The truth won't set us free until we develop the skill, the talent, and the moral courage to use it."

## ~ Emotional Courage ~

Emotional courage requires us to open our emotions and face them (even at the risk of feeling uncomfortable and vulnerable). It can be as simple as confronting our own emotional pain from the past and working to resolve it. It can also be the ability to share our inner feelings with a trusted person, coach, or therapist.

As you know, my grandfather was a war hero, a POW. To many, he was the epitome of brave. He faced extreme suffering and endured war crimes and torture. He was indeed a brave man and soldier; however, his courage was very one-laned. He was trained to be physically and mentally courageous, and he was exemplary, yet he was not equipped with the skills to be emotionally vulnerable (which takes a lot of courage). He certainly wasn't taught about true emotional courage, and, if anything, he deemed it a weakness. To him, emotions were not courageous, but not having any was. It's fair to say, as a society, we have come far in our understanding of emotional courage.

When my husband Dane was at his lowest, being bombarded with suicidal thoughts and ideation, he often fell into the notion that emotional sharing was a weakness. Luckily, he had enough awareness that even through his gravest, hardest, and darkest days, he exerted just a few minutes of emotional and spiritual courage to confide in me. He took a leap of faith into the unknown and exposed his deepest insecurities, and, as his wife, I know how much courage that took.

In the family biographical movie *We Bought a Zoo*, Matt Damon's character, Benjamin Mee, says, "You know, sometimes all you need is twenty seconds of insane courage, just literally twenty seconds of embarrassing bravery, and I promise you something great will come of it."

Well, I can attest this is true. My husband took his 20 seconds of insane courage, and it altered the trajectory of our life. He confessed how low and dark his thoughts had become. He admitted that he needed help, and he had the courage to face the demons that were tormenting his psyche. As Ralph Waldo Emerson said, "A hero is no braver than an ordinary man, but he is braver five minutes longer."

Emotional courage isn't easy; in fact, it's deeply challenging for most of us. Let's look at the emotions and feelings they trigger ... Do they make you feel uncomfortable?

**Love.** Showing love, declaring love, giving love, being in love, risking love, receiving love.

**Shame or hurt.** Sharing shame and hurt, admitting shame and hurt, owning the hurt we have caused, releasing guilt.

**Forgiveness.** Forgiving someone, forgiving yourself, asking for forgiveness, reconciling past hurts, and moving forward.

**Guilt.** Releasing guilt, remembering past guilt, forgiving a "guilty" person, forgiving yourself for things you feel guilty about.

**Desire.** Accepting desire, channeling ambition, recognizing your sexual desire, recognizing the shadow side of too much desire or ambition.

The list of emotions goes on.

The research is clear: suppressing and denying our fundamental emotions leads to emotional instability and serious health issues. Finding a healthy and safe way to take care of our emotional health is vital to thriving.

This means not denying our positive emotions either. Many people feel more at home with pangs of depression and anxiety than they do with joy and ecstasy. We can become accustomed to sharing our struggles and can forget our positive emotions. We must make room for positive emotions, as they are fundamental to our overall health.

We must take off our well-worn social masks and allow ourselves to be truly seen.

## ~ Intellectual Courage ~

Cultivating intellectual courage is our ability to question our thinking and challenge our assumptions, as well as engaging in discussions about difficult topics or complex ideas. It can also be the courage to look at opposing viewpoints and research and engage with others in an intellectual debate.

Researchers and experts in critical and fair-minded thinking Dr. Richard Paul and Dr. Linda Elder outline what they deem intellectual courage:

*Intellectual courage may be defined as having a consciousness of the need to face and fairly address ideas, beliefs or viewpoints toward which one has strong negative emotions and to which one has not given a serious hearing. Intellectual courage is connected to the recognition that ideas that society considers dangerous or absurd are sometimes rationally justified (in whole or in part) ... People need courage to be fair-minded thinkers in these circumstances. The penalties for nonconformity can be severe.*[4]

Challenging our own intellectual understanding can be like running our nails down a blackboard, but I believe we must investigate the places we don't dare look in order to know who we are, what we stand for, and why.

I have also discovered that some people hide their true intellect. They play dumb to avoid the spotlight or looking "too bigheaded" with their intellectual prowess. Sadly, I see this in many women. Culturally and historically, women have been silenced and their voices suppressed. Many girls and women have been denied a basic education and therefore denied the ability to exercise their intellect or even discuss basic philosophy.[5] Throughout history, females have had to fight for basic human rights, and in doing so we have learned to suppress our intellectual capacity to "fit in" or avoid being disruptive or challenging. Thank God for all the women who didn't play that game. Because of them, we are writing a new story.

One of my clients, who we will call Arya, was one such woman. She didn't realize that she was always denying her intellectual powers. She was a *very* smart woman with many accolades and achievements but whenever someone commented on her intellectual prowess, she always dismissed them. She would say things like, "I'm not that smart. I just stayed at college a long, long time." She was naturally sweet and humble, and she refused to accept her intellectual gifts. When I would ask her professional opinion on something, she often balked, answering directly but ending with, "… but I may be wrong, as that's just my opinion."

One day, I challenged her on her continually dismissive behavior. I asked her why she always denied her gifts and refused to accept compliments about her intellect. She was shocked! She didn't even realize she did that. It was totally unconscious (until I made it conscious for her). When she realized it, she gasped (literally gasped!). Tears sprung from her eyes.

She confessed that in the culture she grew up in, the boys and men were often asked the questions, not the women. Although she considered herself an empowered woman, she was taught to be polite and sweet and not "show off" her sharp mind. She was conditioned to be intellectually submissive so she would still be considered worthy of marriage (yes, it's hard to read). She didn't realize that, as a grown woman, she was still unconsciously hiding her gifts like she was taught.

When she saw the cycle in herself and her behavior, she consciously began to use her intellect, and the results were outstanding! Arya rose to her potential and never went back to her old unconscious habits. She knew that to break her ancestral heritage and the societal conditioning she had been exposed to, she needed to be a role model, not a statistic.

## ᨆ Spiritual Courage ᨆ

Cultivating spiritual courage is important in the areas of our faith, belief, and life's purpose. It's about staying true to our spiritual values and beliefs regardless of circumstances. Many religious leaders have had to exercise spiritual courage to stay true to their Higher Power. The stories of Jesus and Buddha both show the threads of spiritual courage. Buddha defied his wealthy upbringing and father's orders to leave the palace walls, and Jesus defied Jewish traditions to bring his message of love and faith to humanity.

Shamans and ancient warriors have long spoken of the need for spiritual courage, and many rituals and ceremonies they performed helped cultivate strength and bravery. I believe that undertaking your own spiritual quest takes courage. It's a wild and unpredictable journey that, once you step onto, you can't get off. For that reason, we need an environment that supports our beliefs to help them remain strong within us.

Some clients have shared their secret spiritual beliefs with me because they feel stuck in the spiritual closet and afraid to share their beliefs with those closest to them. This can be really tough, as the soul needs a sacred place in which to share. For many, sharing their spirituality with family or friends threatens their sense of safety and belonging. I know of many family conflicts that have occurred over a difference in spiritual understanding or a change of faith.

I believe that we all need a "spiritual home" in which we belong, and, for some people, they need to find it outside of their family home. This doesn't mean we all need to belong to a religious group or spiritual community; it means we need a person or two with whom we can share our sacred self. This can be a teacher, a coach, a person we meet at a retreat, or a like-minded support person who allows us to simply be ourselves. Opening up your sacredness can at first feel vulnerable, which is why it's important to find those who you can trust with your spiritual center. Finding these people can take spiritual courage, but if sharing and expressing your spiritual self is important to you, then it's worth the effort.

Online communities like ours can also be a wonderful way to connect with like-minded people, and there are numerous webinars and meditation groups to choose from. For me personally, I draw a lot of inspiration from my spiritual practices and in being around like-minded and faith-filled people. I love to share my sacred spirituality in a heart-centered and trusted environment and lead people to discovering theirs for themselves.

 Scan the QR code to gain 24-7 access to the Bloom Portal and be part of the renowned community full of like-minded women all RISING to greatness together.

I believe that spiritual courage leads to transformation. Having the courage to own your faith and act in accordance with what keeps you strong is deeply important to your wellbeing and those around you. As the ancient sage Lao Tzu said, "If you want to awaken all of humanity, then awaken all of yourself. If you want to eliminate the suffering in the world, then eliminate all that is dark and negative in yourself. Truly, the greatest gift you have to give is that of your own self-transformation."

## Courage Exercise

Look at the six aspects of courage and pick one that would benefit you most. Where do you need more courage?

Which place would courage serve you most? Do you need courage to make a business decision or a relationship or financial decision? Do you want more social confidence? Do you need more courage to be true to yourself, or take a risk by opening up your emotional courage?

Anaïs Nin said, "Life shrinks or expands in proportion to one's courage."

Where would you like to **expand** your life right now?

## Physical Courage

*Do you need more physical courage?*

.................................................................................................................

*How would physical courage best serve you?*

.................................................................................................................

.................................................................................................................

.................................................................................................................

.................................................................................................................

.................................................................................................................

.................................................................................................................

*How can you begin to create more physical courage?*

## Social Courage
*Where specifically do you need to cultivate more social courage?*

*What small actions can you take to cultivate more social courage?*

..............................................................................................................................

..............................................................................................................................

..............................................................................................................................

..............................................................................................................................

..............................................................................................................................

..............................................................................................................................

..............................................................................................................................

..............................................................................................................................

..............................................................................................................................

..............................................................................................................................

*Who is a safe person to help you cultivate more social courage?*

..............................................................................................................................

..............................................................................................................................

..............................................................................................................................

..............................................................................................................................

..............................................................................................................................

..............................................................................................................................

*Was there a past incident or trauma that disrupted your social growth? How did this affect you?*

*What would you gain by being more socially courageous?*

........................................................................................................

........................................................................................................

........................................................................................................

........................................................................................................

........................................................................................................

........................................................................................................

........................................................................................................

........................................................................................................

## Moral Courage

*Where in your life do you need to be more morally courageous?*

........................................................................................................

........................................................................................................

........................................................................................................

........................................................................................................

........................................................................................................

........................................................................................................

........................................................................................................

........................................................................................................

*What is stopping you from exhibiting more moral courage?*

*How would cultivating more moral courage serve you and the people around you?*

*What actions can you take to cultivate more moral courage?*

..................................................................................................

..................................................................................................

..................................................................................................

..................................................................................................

..................................................................................................

..................................................................................................

..................................................................................................

..................................................................................................

## Emotional Courage

*Where do you need to be more emotionally courageous?*

..................................................................................................

..................................................................................................

..................................................................................................

..................................................................................................

..................................................................................................

..................................................................................................

..................................................................................................

..................................................................................................

*What actions can you take to begin to cultivate more emotional courage?*

*Who is a safe person to help you cultivate more emotional courage?*

*What emotions are you avoiding?*

..................................................................................................................

..................................................................................................................

..................................................................................................................

..................................................................................................................

..................................................................................................................

..................................................................................................................

..................................................................................................................

*What emotions would you like to express more often?*

..................................................................................................................

..................................................................................................................

..................................................................................................................

..................................................................................................................

..................................................................................................................

..................................................................................................................

..................................................................................................................

..................................................................................................................

..................................................................................................................

## Intellectual Courage

*Are there areas (often opposing your point of view) that you need to examine to be more intellectually courageous?*

........................................................................................................
........................................................................................................
........................................................................................................
........................................................................................................
........................................................................................................

*Are you extremely biased in some areas of your life or with some specific topics that are causing angst in your relationships?*

........................................................................................................
........................................................................................................
........................................................................................................
........................................................................................................
........................................................................................................
........................................................................................................
........................................................................................................
........................................................................................................
........................................................................................................

*Are you deliberately avoiding your intellect and "playing dumb" out of fear?*

..................................................................................................................

*Are you hiding your intellectual prowess?*

..................................................................................................................

*Are you using your intellect to avoid your emotions?*

..................................................................................................................

*Where can you begin to cultivate intellectual courage?*

..................................................................................................................

..................................................................................................................

..................................................................................................................

..................................................................................................................

..................................................................................................................

..................................................................................................................

..................................................................................................................

..................................................................................................................

..................................................................................................................

## Spiritual Courage

*Are you needing to lean into your faith and cultivate more spiritual courage?*

*Are you in the spiritual closet and keeping your spiritual life secret to avoid others' opinions? If so, why?*

*Are you ready to develop your spiritual powers and use them? If so, what steps would you take?*

*What could you do to cultivate more spiritual courage?*

> "And most important, have the courage to follow your heart and intuition. They somehow already know what you truly want to become. Everything else is secondary."
> —STEVE JOBS

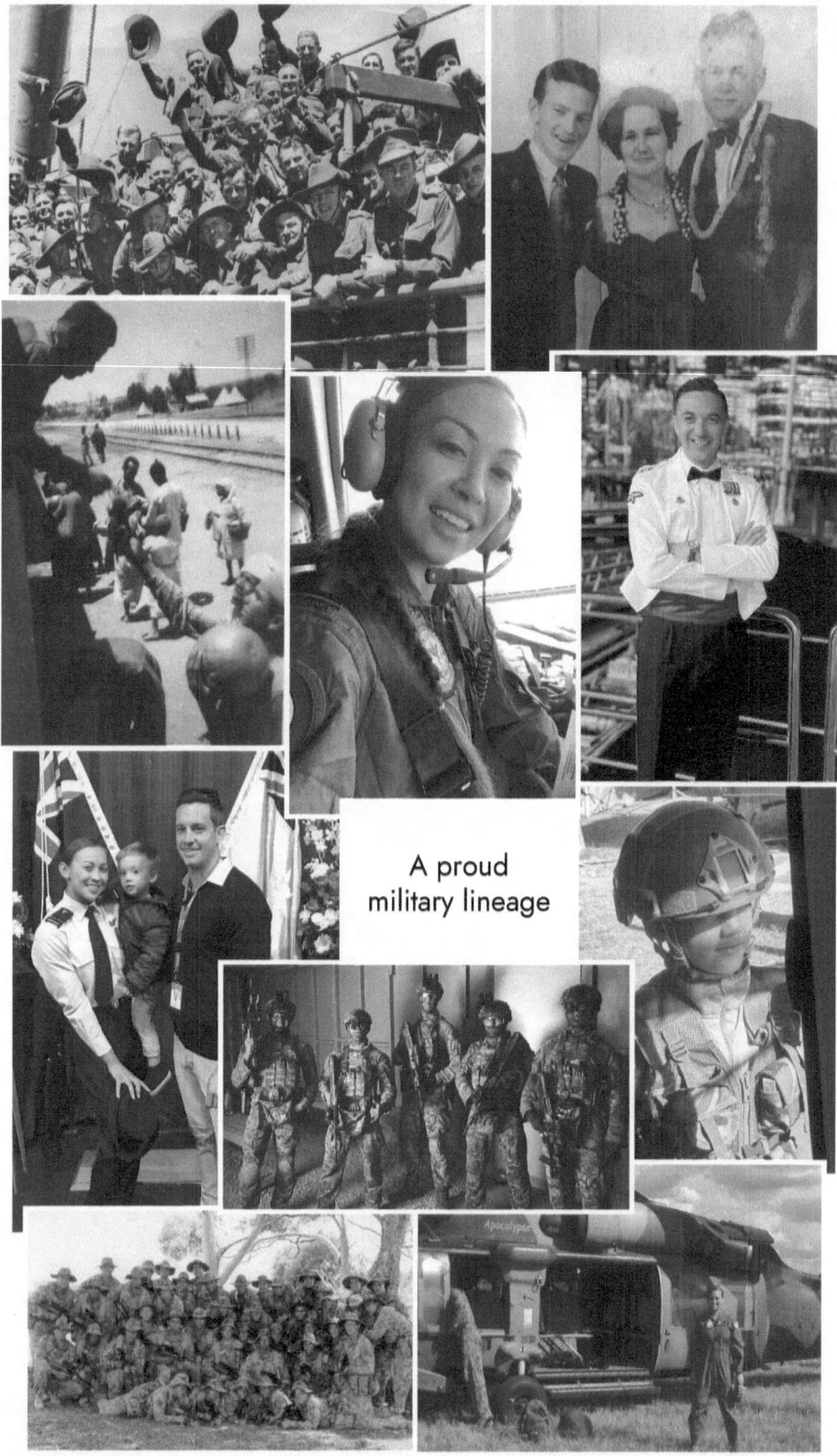

A proud military lineage

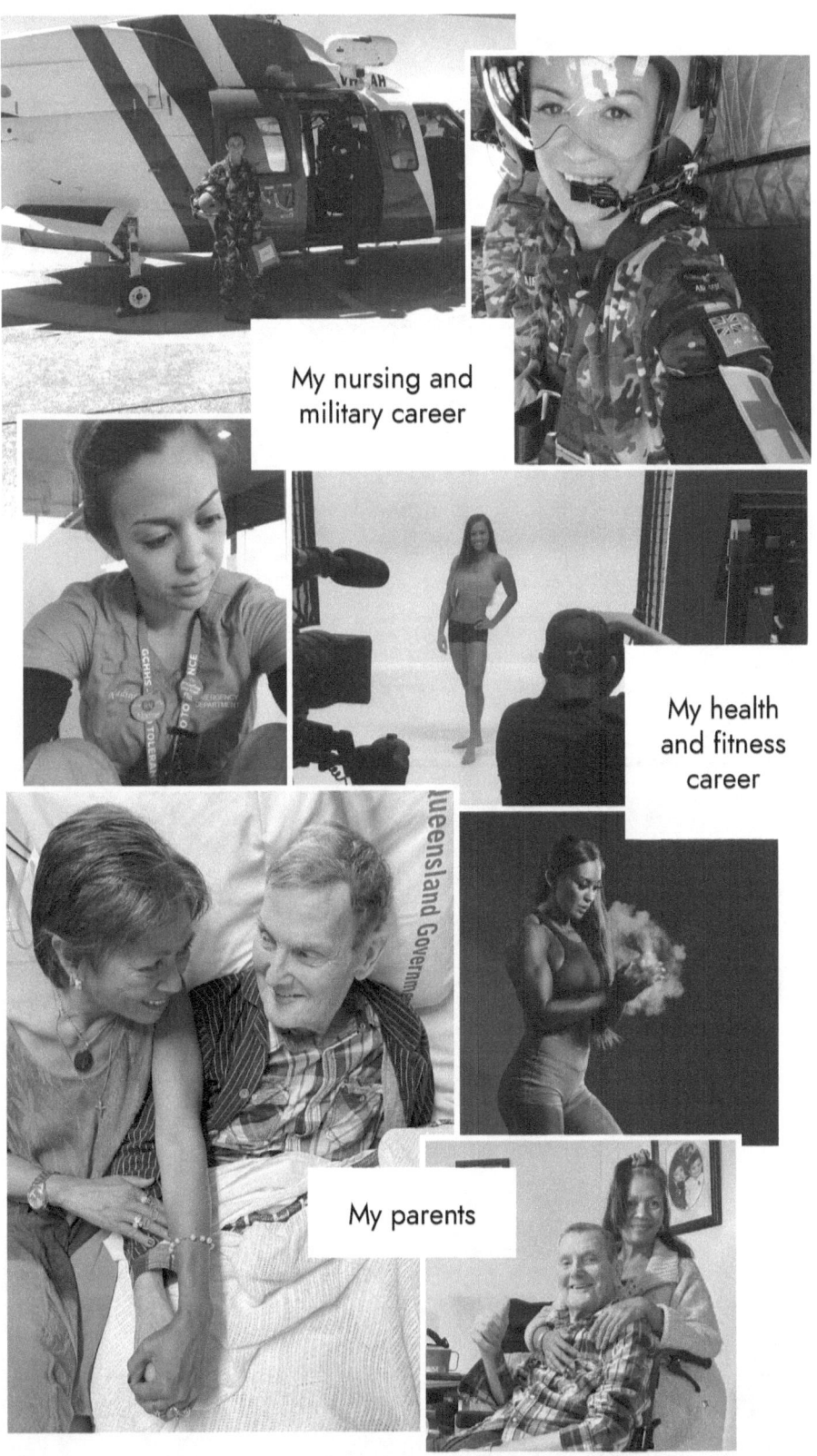

"Our individual consciousness
is always expanding, and
we are always upgrading to
the next version of our self.
It's a continual cycle of
rebirth and growth, and
it's rarely a straight road."

—NADINE MULLER

CHAPTER 6

# THE DARK AND LIGHT OF LIFE

I believe we never fully arrive. People are looking to the nth degree to say, "I've made it! I've reached the summit"—but then the next part of their journey begins. It's like a ladder: the moment you have one foot firmly on a step, the other foot is in the air searching to take the next step.

We are in flux, experiencing continual evolution, and we never stay stagnant or firmly planted at a specific point called "arrival." We just pause momentarily until the next part of our evolution begins.

Life never stays the same, and neither do we. You aren't the same person you were in your childhood or teens because, along the way, you had experiences that shaped you and the way you perceive the world. You didn't need to try to grow;

it just happened organically, independent of your thoughts or beliefs about it.

As a species, human beings have evolved and changed. The Earth cycles, and seasons are in a perpetual state of death and renewal. Life itself is a full-blown experience of adapting, changing, and evolving. You are not independent of this, and neither am I. I guess we have to come to grips with the fact that change is the only constant. We never fully arrive at "destination perfection," and we never stay in one place too long.

Recently, I have found myself gobsmacked at my life (in the best possible way). I often say to Dane, "I can't believe how amazing our freedom life is!" The fact that I have a successful purpose-led mission and heart-led business, a beautiful supportive family, healthy children, an incredible work team, inspiring friendships, and spend my time traveling domestically and internationally full-time while running a multi-seven-figure company blows my freakin' mind. I also know that life will always do what life does best ... and things will change. It doesn't mean they will change for the worse, but they will change. We must equip ourselves to adapt and not hold on to our "arrival points" too tightly.

In saying that, we also need to honor and celebrate our incredible efforts when we do accomplish a dream or a goal. It's a balancing act, the ladder of life.

> *"A bend in the road is not the end of the road ... unless you fail to make the turn."*
> —HELEN KELLER

## The Staircase of Success

It's important to honor all the versions of ourselves and all the phases we grew through (even those that make us cringe). All those changes (including weird phases and bad hairdos) made us who we are today. Even the trauma and the brutal and ugly parts of our situations or psyches gave us a lesson or a learning or two.

No matter how resistant we are to change, it will happen anyway. We just gotta accept it as a law of life. Even our mortal bodies change, whether or not we consent, and no matter how much Botox or surgery we have, we can't fully prevent the aging process that happens on the inside. We are doomed by nature to change and adapt. That's why the ancient Greek philosopher Heraclitus's quote, "There is nothing permanent except change," is still posted regularly on Insta today.

When a mentor of mine challenged the way I was always *striving to arrive*, I was at first a little shocked. Unconsciously, I was constantly on a mission to arrive somewhere. A future place I deemed "better" than where I was. I was hell-bent on "making it" to that invisible point that I believed was *the* point I needed to get to. The summit of so-called success.

Strangely, when I did arrive there, I was only momentarily

excited ... and before I realized it, my brain started to conjure up my next arrival point, my next mission, my next adventure and evolution.

When my mentor stated, "Nadine, you will never fully arrive at your final destination and remain there," my brain kind of paused in a suspended state of shock. A wave of warm relief coursed through my body, as I knew he was speaking truth. It was like I had just received a permission slip to relax and accept that I was, in fact, taking a series of steps that led to the next step. I was walking up a staircase, and each step represented a landing where I needed to celebrate and reflect.

In fact, we are all walking up our own divine staircase of life. Sometimes, we slip down a step and need to gather our balance again. Other times, we skip a step, jumping up two.

So, when I got off the frantic hamster wheel and stopped chasing the final summit, I changed my relationship with time and effort. I kept the summit as my ultimate vision but focused on making the next rung, the next step. When my mentor said, "You'll never fully arrive and stay there," something in me clicked. My hamster wheel became a divine staircase, and I could walk up it at my own pace, stopping on a step when I wanted to enjoy the scenery. I finally began to enjoy each step and the process without the desperation of wanting to arrive quickly. Just as American actress Lily Tomlin once said, "The road to success is always under construction," the staircase to success is never completed. I believe we build it on the way, bit by bit, nail by nail, step by step.

The great thing about climbing your staircase to success is that it's yours! You define what each step is and how long you want to rest on the way to your dreams. You don't even need to have an "ultimate vision" of the summit if you can't see one. You can simply take one step at a time. As the great civil rights leader Martin Luther King Jr. said, "Take the first step in faith. You don't have to see the whole staircase, just take the first step."

## Winning Moments on Your Staircase

There are always people who have done extraordinary and mind-boggling things. There are business owners who build and create unicorn businesses; there are influencers who have more followers than most people could fathom; there are musical prodigies and incredible athletes with talent oozing out of their pores. But don't scroll social media and compare your unique road to success to theirs. We are all born with our own genius, and we aren't supposed to be the same as anybody else.

Comparison steals your enjoyment and erodes your self-esteem. I celebrate other people's success when I see it, but I don't compare. Celebration is a joy; comparison is a trap.

After that comment from my mentor at the time about never fully arriving, I took a radical mindset shift and started celebrating every small milestone along the way. And what happened? Quite simply—it was a game changer.

Research from acclaimed professor and organizational theorist Karl E. Weick shows that "small wins" in fact help us reduce anxiety and fear, clarify our direction, and increase the likelihood of our future success.[1] Kinda cool, hey? All those little moments actually make you more likely to succeed.

In fact, once I started to feel good about the little wins, I discovered that my old way of being—only focusing on the big moments and massive accomplishments—was undermining my attempts at success. I didn't know there were decades of research showing that major life events, like marriage and employment, didn't have massive impacts on our happiness. In fact, sometimes big moments like getting married or divorced, winning the lottery, losing your job, or buying a red convertible didn't alter the happiness scale for more than a few months.[2] WTF?! Mind warp! And here's why—*we adapt quickly.*

Humans are made to adapt quickly to changing events, both good and bad. Now, you'd think that winning the lottery would guarantee prolonged happiness—but it doesn't! In fact, many winners go back to their emotional baseline within one year, and some end up less happy.[3] Remember what I said back in the beginning chapters about hedonic adaptation? The fact that we often go back to our emotional baseline regardless of circumstance is a big deal. But what guarantees us prolonged joy if the big things don't? It seems that all the research points to what we intuitively feel within …

- The quality of our relationships with family and friends.
- Forgiveness and letting go of negativity and resentment.
- Gratitude and giving.[4]

Small habits and activities that people do consistently over the long run have been found to have a cumulative and longer-lasting effect that hustling toward only big-ass goals.[5] That's why all my strategies for climbing that staircase and rising to your highest dreams and goals include celebrating your small moments, increasing your gratitude for life, and letting go of old resentments and negative thought processes.

## Don't Forget about Quantum Leaps

Celebrating the small steps along the way doesn't mean you won't take quantum leaps. In fact, throughout my life, I have taken massive leaps (leaping over numerous steps all in one go) and have enjoyed that progression.

Quantum leaps often occur after a period of pausing or assuming that nothing is happening. I like to think of it as "collapsing time."

My business took a quantum leap after I began to use mentors and dump my own mindset of needing to do everything myself. Once I started to work on the business more than in it, growth shot through the roof, and profit increased exponentially. Yet it was all those years of hard work, trial and error, and realizing I needed a new approach that created the quantum leap, the time collapse.

When I went through that epic quantum jump, I decided to celebrate it like never before. I early retired my mom, set up her financial future, cleared her of all her financial debts, and sent her on multiple holidays and overseas trips. After decades of hard work and taking care of everyone else, it was her turn to receive. It had always been a pipe dream of mine, and that quantum jump made it a reality. The feeling of achieving that dream is indescribable.

In hindsight, I can see that the achievement was both the result of a series of small steps and one quantum leap, as if all those little steps acted as rocket fuel to launch that dream to its final destination. Therefore, climbing your ladder of success can be a series of small steps forward (and sometimes backward) as well as quantum leaps and moments where you are stationary. Sometimes it can feel more like a spring coil that recoils back just to gain more resistance so it can catapult you forward. Like a bow and arrow does in order to hit its target.

**It doesn't matter how your journey goes, as long as you back yourself during the climb, take moments to celebrate your small wins, and enjoy the scenery along the way.**

*"Life is a journey, not a destination."*
—RALPH WALDO EMERSON

## The Little Birdie on Your Shoulder

As you wander through life doing your best, there will always be a little birdie on our shoulder chirping at you. I have a little birdie of my own. We all do.

It may say things like …

"You're not good enough."

"You're not smart enough."

"You're not pretty enough."

"You're not strong enough."

It can chirp a whole lot of nonsense. Nonsense that you are more likely to believe because that little birdie knows your triggers and insecurities. It knows what you're more likely to believe and bend to.

There will always be inner work to do. Much like the staircase of success, we also have an emotional staircase that never brings us to a final destination. For example, once you've dealt with your past issues, a new issue may arise, and you think, *Fuck, more work to do.*

One of my clients, Bec, had some deep and harsh shit to deal with. She was abused in her childhood and did a lot of inner work to arrive at a point of feeling worthy and being able to trust people again. She delved deeply into inner-child work, and, over time, reclaimed her worth and power. It took huge amounts of emotional endurance to arrive at a point where she could look into a mirror and love the gorgeous woman (and girl inside) looking back at her. It was a beautiful moment when she truly learned to love herself for all her parts.

She went into the trenches of her pain to reclaim the lost parts of herself stolen from her childhood. However, a few months after that, she realized that her relationships had been built through her old lens of being a lost little girl, and she needed to create a new lens and dialogue based on the woman she was today. What did that mean? *More work.*

She had to explore what mattered to her now, what she wanted as an empowered woman rather than a frightened girl. Bec became a woman who loved herself and, therefore, no longer felt like she needed constant validation. She didn't need someone to fulfill her big emotional holes, as she was doing it herself. As a result, her relationship changed, but her partner didn't know why she had changed so suddenly. He wondered why she didn't need him like she once did. He started to feel insecure and worried that maybe she was seeing someone else. Although this wasn't the case, Bec's shift toward empowerment created a vibrational change in their relationship. Bec had shifted. Her inner child wasn't needing what it once needed, and her entire way of thinking and behaving changed.

But kudos to Bec. She saw the ripple effect of this change and didn't revert to old patterns. Instead, she communicated with her partner and reassured him that she was happier than ever, explaining that the "new" her was in fact a blessing for both of them. Bec and her partner then joined our couples mentorship experience and began to build the relationship of their dreams. They shared their fears and their dreams, and, over time, decided to get engaged!

Bec is one example of what "doing the work" really looks like. She didn't settle for a half-lived life. Instead, she understood that doing the work on her shadow self was just as important as embracing her goodness.

> "It's better to light a candle than to curse the darkness."
> —OLD CHINESE PROVERB

## The Continuous Journey

You've probably heard of the Japanese term *kaizen*. The term translates in English to "continuous improvement," and it has been popularized in Western culture and largely used in the corporate world to help build seamless processes and human-centric team culture while continually focusing on improving all aspects of business.

The kaizen philosophy also applies to our personal lives, and it's important to build on the small steps you make rather than strive only for quantum leaps and acceleration.

When I began to apply the principle of continuous improvement, a huge relief swept over me. I also stopped trying to eradicate negative beliefs I held and instead started noticing them and being a compassionate witness to them. They became less intrusive and obsessive, and, in many cases, they started to fade. I also discovered that the little birdie chirping away on my shoulder was often there regardless of my circumstances. It was a pest some days, and other days it was quieter and tame.

You see, we are always evolving. We are evolution in human form. Our individual consciousness is always expanding, and we are always upgrading to the next version of our self. It's a continual cycle of rebirth and growth, and it's rarely a straight road. It's a natural cycle of being human.

**Who you have been, who you are today, and who you will be are all within you.**

You are evolving and growing morning, noon, and night, whether you want to or not. Even if you resist your growth and try in vain to "not change," then life will go ahead and change things for you, whether you want it or not. I believe it's easier and more enjoyable to just work with the universe and its natural cycles of evolution.

One of my clients, Aliyah, worked with me for fourteen months straight. When she joined our community, she was in dire straits, but she said something radical that first day. She said, "Whatever comes up must be whatever I need to look at." Her understanding and ability to see life as a school of awareness and learning was the cornerstone of her dramatic change. She really did the work. She boldly looked at all the things that weren't working in her life and took responsibility for them. She saw them as opportunities for growth. And guess what? Aliyah transformed herself from the inside out. She didn't balk at the growth; she took courage and was willing to go places she'd never gone before. She knew that her past results "mirrored" something she needed to learn, and she took on that learning.

As spiritual writer and teacher Ken Wilber pointed out, "The understanding of 'evolutionary consciousness' is perhaps the most important thing lacking in spiritual practices today. Evolution means growth and development. This means that there are aspects of reality that have not yet arisen in our consciousness. But they will arise if we grow."[6]

Read that last part again—*there are aspects of reality that have not yet arisen in our consciousness.* But here's the kicker—they *will* arise if we grow!

Finding those untapped parts of your consciousness is an exciting adventure. Sure, it can be scary at times, but learning about your inner and authentic self always reaps rewards in the long run. You become more aware of your potential and limitations, more conscious of what holds you back, and more able to release the shackles you bind yourselves with. In short, you set yourself free from being a victim of circumstances and start to become the creator of your destiny.

Spiritual teacher Eckhart Tolle said in *A New Earth*, "Life will give you whatever experience is most helpful for the evolution of your consciousness. How do you know this is the experience you need? Because this is the experience you are having at the moment."[7]

Life is a vibrational match to whatever you need to experience in order to evolve your consciousness. When we truly know this, we can relax and trust that wherever we are and whatever we are experiencing is right for our soul, right now.

## The Law of Polarity: The Dark and Light of Life

Life is full of dichotomies. As human beings, we are at the mercy of extreme events and experiences: life and death, war and peace, love and hate, good and evil, light and dark. We live in a world of paradoxes with opposite forces dancing together.

Learning to accept these opposites as part of our reality is the start of wisdom. Although we would all love to live in a world where nothing bad happens and no duality exists, it's not how the world works. We are, in fact, alive due to the nature of opposite energies: the sun and moon, night and day, winter and summer, male and female—each different yet complementary too.

In Taoist philosophy of Yin and Yang is one of the oldest descriptions of this opposite energy, dating back to the third century BCE. Although it was originally used to describe the way the universe works, it is now widely recognized as the symbol of balance, reflecting that the duality of opposite forces is both complementary and interconnected.

**Yin** represents feminine, passive, dark, creative, and yielding aspects of being.

**Yang** represents masculine, active, light, certainty, and dominant aspects of being.

Together, yin and yang create balance and harmony in the universe and within ourselves and our relationships. They help us understand our inner nature and the harmonious interconnectedness of all things.

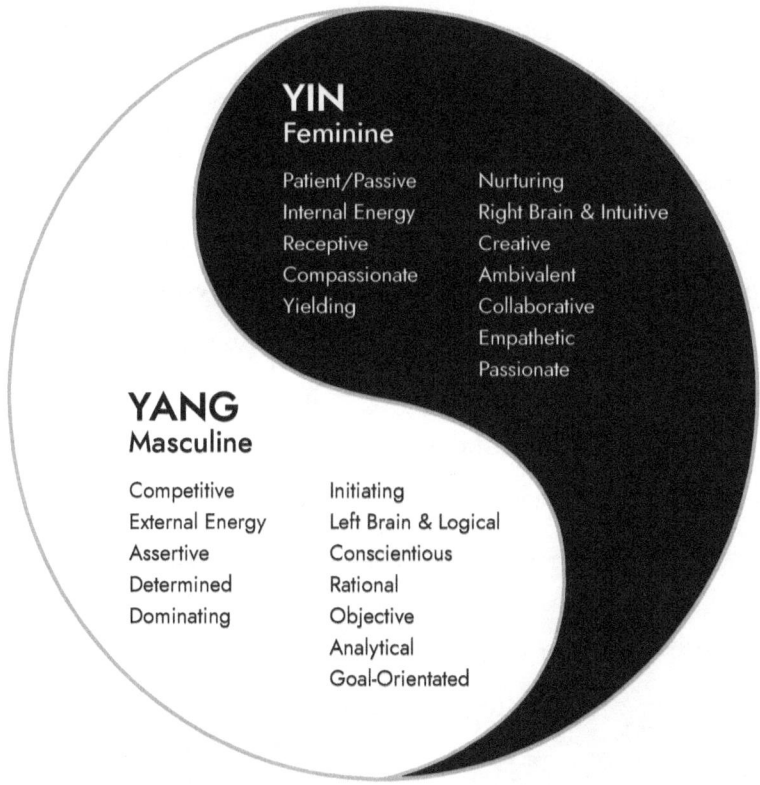

Dr. Carl Jung also discussed the importance of understanding the opposing natures that coexist inside each individual. He called these anima and animus. The *anima* (Latin for soul) represents the feminine aspect of a man's unconscious. The *animus* (Latin for mind or spirit) represents the masculine aspect of a woman's unconscious.

Jung said each transcends the individual's personal psychology and aims to integrate elements of self. The "soul" has a feminine character in a man and a masculine character in a woman. His *anima* wants to reconcile and unite; her *animus* tries to discern and discriminate.[8] They essentially dance the tango together all lifetime, and that's what makes it so sensual, intimate, and dynamic.

These two natures dwell within all of us regardless of our gender or sexuality, and, through self-development and awareness, we can reconcile and balance these energies. The reason why this can be important is that many of us (including myself) have dominant patterns, and we can suppress or neglect the masculine or feminine sides of our psyche. This can lead to relationship issues and interpersonal conflicts that present themselves in behaviors and attitudes.

### Masculine energy

Represents: confidence, structure, action, decisiveness, and clarity.

- **In the positive:** The masculine aspects within help us plan and go forward with our goals with stability and intention. The masculine ignites motivation and action and is clear and directive.
- **Lacking:** When we lack masculine energy, we often struggle with focus and direction and lack clear aims and motivation. We tend to struggle with reaching goals and can become apathetic.

- **Excess**: In contrast, too much masculine energy can lead to increased aggression or confrontation, as well as pushing limits and being overly analytical or rigid.

### Feminine energy

Represents: creativity, fluidity, nurturing, and intuitive flair.

- **In the positive:** The feminine aspects within help us remain sensitive, flexible, and compassionate while surrendering and relinquishing control. The feminine helps us tap into our creativity and intuition.
- **Lacking:** When we lack feminine energy, we can "block" ourselves emotionally from others and become unbalanced and out of touch with our creativity and intuition. We can disconnect from feeling deeply and put up a shield to deflect the flow of life and its vast spacious energy.
- **Excess:** In contrast, too much feminine energy can lead to codependency, victimhood, and a lack of healthy boundaries. It can also impede action and invite lethargy and feeling down.

In many ways, we have a culture that idolizes the masculine. We admire the hustle culture and "doing" rather than being. We give awards to those who can build the tallest buildings and win the biggest championships, and, in many ways, we have squeezed the feminine out of the modern world in pursuit of building more, becoming more, and doing more. Now, all those aspects are important and noble qualities, and we must have them. However, dominant masculine energy in a culture can easily push out the more subtle and nourishing qualities of the gentler feminine. And thus, an imbalance grows.

Until I learned about energetics, my marriage with Dane was on the brink of collapse. I was so masculine-dominant in my energy, with Dane in his wounded masculine, that we just butted heads and found problems with each other. There was no polarity between us. I didn't feel safe to step into my feminine energy because I was holding up the household with my strength and action-orientated ways. I didn't have the luxury to soften into my feminine when we needed my strength to survive. Dane was battling his own mental demons and was fluctuating between anger and depression and unworthiness in ways that I didn't have the capacity to handle at the time. Our intimacy reflected the lack of energetic polarity, and we found ourselves less sexually intimate than before.

Our dual energetics were a recipe for disaster, and we were heading down a dark road. When we learned about energetics and polarity, it changed everything. I recognized my overcompensatory behavior and saw how I was saturating my life in sheer masculine energy. Allowing myself to drop into my feminine energy was a game changer. I didn't realize that, in many ways, I was demasculinizing my husband and exhausting myself. But this was before I fully understood the laws of polarity in relationships.

In relationships, polarity is the masculine and feminine. They are two opposing energies that magnetically attract each other. If two people are both energetically masculine, the poles repel. If two people are both energetically feminine, they also repel. The magnet force attracts through the law of polarity. Just like a sensual tango, someone is dancing forward, and someone is dancing backward to make it one seamless display of unity and effortless grace.

Now remember, this isn't about being a male or female, or about being in a heterosexual relationship; gay couples experience the same issues with polarity too. It's about understanding the polarity of energy that exists within us as an individual and then within couples. As author Shakti Gawain said, "The union of feminine and masculine energies within the individual is the basis of all creation."

Your responsibility within your relationships (both with yourself and your partner) is to see your patterns, balance the energy of opposites, and integrate it into your relationships and life.

> "There is a collective force rising up on the earth today, an energy of the reborn feminine."
> —MARIANNE WILLIAMSON

## Your Mess Becomes Your Message

Once Dane and I did the inner work on ourselves and corrected our imbalances within, this naturally led to more polarity, deeper intimacy, higher amounts of appreciation, and finally communicating once and for all, seeing and hearing each other. It was like magic! I couldn't help but wonder how many couples separated or divorced based on not knowing about the dynamics of energetics and polarity.

We decided to expand in this area of our professional development, create our own bodies of work, share our experiences and help other couples rise from those similar challenges that many modern-day couples face. We began a couple's retreat experience called United, which helped couples unpack the issues, discover the root causes, heal intergenerational wounds, understand polarity, and show up in a new revolutionary way. I remember looking over at Dane during the event and feeling absolute admiration for him. Here was a man willing to go into the trenches of his psyche, willing to dive into the raw messiness of our relationship issues and embrace a new way of relating to his wife, and then sharing that journey with other couples.

It dawned on me that, in that moment, we had made the mess our message. We had risen from the basement of despair and found a new story.

Sure, it took a hell of a lot of work from both of us to own our shadows and take responsibility for our part in the mess, but we cleaned our shit up together. When you both roll your sleeves up and are willing to get down and dirty with the realness of your relationship, miracles can happen. I kid you not.

I have seen couples go from the brink of divorce to wanting to rip each other's clothes off and make passionate love within hours! That may sound like an exaggeration—but it's not. Why? Because the law of polarity is a magnetic field that attracts and repels according to your energy. Get the polarity of the masculine and feminine energy and its natural law, and—boom! You have instant attraction. Unbreakable energy that pulls together.

Now, of course, some couples have huge issues that can't be solved on the spot. But learning about the masculine and feminine parts of our psyche certainly helps them understand why they got into a bind in the first place. Even repairing your relationship after an affair or betrayal of trust is possible with the right tools and attitude. Since that first retreat, we've held countless more and have guided countless couples all around the world both online and face-to-face.

Scan the QR code for simple yet effective couples' tools and resources for you and your relationship.

Dane and I have been gobsmacked by how many couples can reach a point of maturity when they finally understand the behavior and actions of their partner. We have even seen some couples decide to separate with the most loving hearts because they both dug deep and became real with each other. They both admitted that they never wanted to stay in the relationship. It's radical, right?

Showing up, being real, and doing the work is all it takes to transform your life and your relationship. That's the key to rising I speak about over and over again. The steps are easy, but the deeper work is hard.

Here's a reminder of the process ...

**1. See the shadows**
Identify your energetic patterns. Where are you dominant or lacking? What energy is in excess and how does this affect your relationship?

**2. Balance the energies**
Learn new ways of behaving to balance the dominant, lacking, or excessive energy. Work with your partner to develop new patterns.

**3. Integrate into your life and relationships**
Integration is like a dance. Sometimes it can mean

> taking two steps forward and two steps backward. Learning how to integrate new energy patterns and behavior takes time and effort. However, integrating this into your love life is worth it.

## Ruin or Rise?

One couple we met were in a huge stalemate within their relationship. Kim was a working mom of three children and was self-medicating to hide her depressive episodes. Every time she tried to talk to her husband Paul about how she was feeling, he would roll his eyes as if to say, "Here we go again!" She put up a wall to protect herself and "not let him in" so she wouldn't feel rejected by him.

He was a busy tradesman who would come home exhausted and just wanted to relax at home and not have more shit to deal with. Anytime Paul showed interest in intimacy, Kim would feel angry. After all, he didn't show any love when she was hurting, only when he wanted sex. She pushed him away to protect her feelings. She didn't want to feel like a sex object; she wanted to feel love and intimacy. Paul took her rejection without asking any deeper questions and started pulling away and watching porn behind her back. It became a recipe for absolute disaster, and the hurt and pain was stockpiling, ready for a catastrophic explosion.

Dane and I could see the pattern clearly. Neither of them was communicating what was really going on. Both were hiding from each other and not feeling safe to express their feelings. Both felt unloved by their partner, even though they did love each other.

It took about three hours to change. Kim couldn't speak without crying. Paul was answering in monotone answers and not giving much away. They were protecting themselves and not wanting to hurt the other with truth.

We coached them with effective tools and resources that they now have for life and how to be on the same script of music with communication methods that actually work! Kim admitted that she wanted to be intimate with Paul, but she was hurting from being shunned on an emotional level. Paul looked visibly shocked. He didn't realize his lack of care in the small things (like care and listening) resulted in Kim withholding intimacy (a big thing in his mind). To Kim, it was obvious. She admitted she was self-medicating to cope with her suppressed feelings, and Paul admitted he was watching porn to cope with rejection and the lack of affection and intimacy. They were both medicating their pain.

After many rounds of tears and truth telling, we educated Kim and Paul on the principles of polarity. We showed Paul what it looked like to be emotionally attentive and how to do "small loving touches" and attentive listening to show Kim he cared. We showed Kim what it looked like to allow Paul into her feminine space. Paul needed to step into his masculine energy at home (not just at work) in order to allow Kim to feel held and safe within his presence.

Over time, Kim and Paul kept taking small steps in their relationship. They communicated more and made time to connect and touch and be attentive to each other's energy. They called us for a few more coaching sessions and pieced their relationship back together using the divine dance of masculine and feminine principles. We ensured that they went through the stages of: 1) seeing the shadows, 2) balancing the energies, and 3) integrating it into life.

Last time we saw them, they were giggling like newlyweds and were going strong. Every time they had a setback, they went back to the work we taught them, the tools and resources they now have for life, their united tool kits and strategies, and integrated the wisdom back into their marriage. It had a happy ending because they made their mess their masterpiece. They transformed themselves and their marriage.

## Extraordinary in the Ordinary

Kim and Paul not only rediscovered each other, but they also rediscovered the joy of finding the extraordinary in the ordinary.

Filling life with awe and wonder and breathtaking moments is the juice in life. We all know how quickly life can change. How brutal it can be, and how beautiful it can be. How challenging, and how divine. Those dichotomies never stop, but we can always choose the lens we see through.

You can be in a really ordinary place in life and still marvel at the extraordinariness of it. When we decided to sell our house, buy a van, and travel with the kids, homeschooling them along the way, I remember feeling a pinch of *I can't believe we just did that*. I thought of the times we camped in tents as kids and looked up at the star-filled sky, gasping at the galaxy above. Life seemed huge, and I felt so small in comparison. It was beautifully humbling to feel like a tiny speck of life in the scope of the entire solar system. My dad would have marveled at the van. It would have been such a dream for him. But being in tents back in the early days meant I was exposed to night skies and not hotel ceilings. Our dad's basic income gave me riches, and I got to see the extraordinary in the ordinary.

That's why we still carry our swags and tents in the van. We pop them up and revel in these extraordinary ordinary moments. We do it so our kids have these same little moments. The awe and wonder that makes life truly rich.

Keeping this mindset has always kept me optimistic and hopeful when times were hard. Just like the way a little flower pushes through the cement to radiate its beauty, so too does this mindset push through hard times and radiate the beauty that still exists.

These tiny moments of awe and reverence shaped my mind. Kept me believing in the mysterious miracles that life could offer. Although I was small, I could sense that life was huge, which meant I could see and experience grand things in my lifetime. It meant there were no limits to what was possible.

You can do this in all areas of life. Your career, relationships, parenting, finances, and even your relationship with yourself can be nourished by looking at them with the lens of love and appreciation.

Because life is unpredictable and uncertain, we must look for ways to embrace and celebrate its glorious beauty and exquisite moments. It's the simplicity in life that makes it so special.

Here are some simple things I love ...

- A spontaneous smile from a stranger
- A good belly laugh
- The smell of fresh coffee with Vegemite on toast
- The way Dane looks at me when we are approaching each other from a distance
- My kids' imaginative story time at night
- Dance parties as a family whenever, wherever
- Shooting stars blazing through the night sky
- My mom's freshly cooked Filipino dishes
- The sound of waves rhythmically lapping at the shore
- Remembering the clear lucid look in my dad's eyes before he crossed over

Before we move on to the next chapter, take some time to reflect on the extraordinary ordinary moments in your life.

*What are the extraordinary ordinary moments you have lived?*

*What moments open up your heart to awe and gratitude?*

> "We must lean into love when life feels like it will break us. It's the only medicine."
>
> —NADINE MULLER

CHAPTER 7

# CAREGIVING

Regardless of your goals in life, your best-laid plans are going to be disrupted whether you like it or not! At some point, you're going to need to take care of others, whether it's your children, your friends, your partner, your pets, or your aging parents. Life is going to throw some mega curveballs, and that often involves caregiving.

I'm not going to apologize for disrupting the flow of this book to talk about caregiving … because that's exactly what happens in life. Without warning, we are thrust into uncharted territory and become caretakers of others. It's a part of life we rarely look at before it happens.

One of my beautiful clients, Belinda, found herself caring for her best friend with stage-four breast cancer and her elderly father with dementia, while juggling a business and two kids (one with autism). Yep, caregiving ain't for the fainthearted, and it can either be something you see coming or something that lands abruptly and unexpectedly at your doorstep.

US first lady Rosalynn Carter once said, "There are only four kinds of people in the world: those who have been caregivers, those who are currently caregivers, those who will be caregivers, and those who will need caregivers."

I hate to be the one to bear the shitty news—but she's right! We must come to terms with this and get prepared. That means finding resources to draw from, support to lean on, and advocating for both caregivers and receivers, knowing that fate often determines which role you're thrust into first.

Let's firstly make an important distinction—there are two types of caregivers:

- **Formal caregivers:** paid workers in the care providing industry, for example, aged-care workers, palliative care nurses, and disability support workers.
- **Informal caregivers:** unpaid carers usually a spouse, family member, or friend involved in taking care of a loved one's medical requirements, tasks, and daily living requirements.

Given my history of being an emergency and critical care registered nurse, I was more than qualified to take care of Dad. But I did so on an informal basis, as a caring daughter. My professional training certainly helped prepare me, but it didn't make me bulletproof to the emotional toll it takes to be a full-time carer of someone you adore.

Although both types of caregivers are angels in my eyes, I will largely focus on the informal caregiver, as this role doesn't come with training, and people can find themselves thrown into the deep end, suddenly dealing with medical responsibilities, activities of daily living, and personal care. I can tell you that showering your aging and frail dad, helping someone to the toilet, or administering medication to your ill and frightened friend isn't something you've practiced a lot before. It's a whole other ball game.

I found myself in the primary role of caregiver when, along with my dad's dementia in steep decline, he then suffered a significant stroke that he was lucky to survive. It saw him wheelchair-bound, with complete left-side paralysis. To put it lightly, Mom was already overwhelmed with carer's exhaustion before the stroke when Dad was more able-bodied, so boy did this throw a spanner in the works.

My dad—the strong-willed and resilient man—was soon heavily dependent on his family. His independence was stripped from him inch by inch, month by month, year by year, and, before we knew it, we were left with a man whose memory was mostly a blur and needed a high level of care.

Dad had a long battle with dementia, which meant Mom had a long battle in caring for him. She was his primary carer for over a decade, and he wanted to stay at home for as long as possible. Exhausting all support and resources available, it was a slippery slope. We all did our best to grant him his wish for as long as humanly possible. It was a wild ride involving one undeniable family force operating from LOVE, even when everything was crumbling.

## Reality Slap

I remember the first time I noticed Dad's dementia. I was in my final year of high school, and, being school captain, I was delivering a speech at the school assembly and awards.

He came up and celebrated with me, but he called me by my stepsister's name (his eldest daughter from his former marriage). Weeks later, he came to my school classroom to pick me up for an appointment in the city, and when he knocked on the classroom door to collect me, again he spoke to my teacher asking for the wrong person—my other stepsister. I was embarrassed and taken aback by him mixing up his daughters. He was clearly not in his right state of mind.

My friends were often at our house, and my parents were like second parents to many of them, so when this happened in front of my friends, they noticed. It was one of the first major signs that things were getting weird. I could no longer pretend everything was fine.

It was around this time that Dad was attending frequent medical appointments, getting repeat blood tests, and already living with a diagnosis of leukemia and an aortic aneurysm. His health was in a negative spiral, and we weren't necessarily looking for dementia while he was dealing with so many other health issues.

His GP was very proactive and could see his physical and cognitive decline as the cascade of diagnoses stacked against one very ill human. While the decline didn't happen overnight, it felt like it did. Dad went from forgetting things here and there, to being regularly confused, to forgetfulness and confusion becoming the new normal. It was hard to see such a strong and proud man begin to mumble to himself, forget names and faces, and even start to get lost in his own home and town, where he had lived for the past fifteen years.

At the time, we all just took it on the chin and rallied around him. I could see the silent and intrusive forces that culminated and added to Dad's decline—the past alcohol abuse, the domestic violence, his traumatic childhood, his dad's suicide that he witnessed, the ongoing bouts of depression, unresolved trauma, and the string of fractured relationships. I could almost read his mind; he was consumed with worry about dying and what Mom would do without him, leaving us with financial struggle, being a burden on the family, not having lived the life he was capable of living, and leaving us with debt and grief. His neurology was not only malfunctioning, but it was also jammed with worries.

His decline was a long and sad series of events that had started many years before. A career in the Australian Military meant I was away from family a lot, although growing up I was confronted with sporadic violent episodes where Dad, in bouts of significant alcohol abuse, would put Mom and us kids in the firing line. Decades of destructive behavioral patterns, screaming matches between my parents that lasted nights on end, frequent confronting and heart-wrenching scenes—us kids witnessed it all, felt it all, experienced it all. As I grew from a young girl to a teen, and indeed through to my adulthood, I often willingly put myself in the firing line to defend what I knew was right, knowing this behavior was absolutely unacceptable, even if the aggressor was someone I loved and adored—my own father.

This time in our lives was an absolute roller-coaster ride, with unresolved intergenerational trauma and togetherness aplenty. A strange combination I know—but often such opposites walk together, forging a path of reconciliation.

Over time, Dad's health continued to decline, and Mom was adamant she would stand by her husband of almost four decades, doing the best she could, with her family supporting her. However, we all knew we needed to find a more sustainable path forward. Gradually, it became apparent that we needed significant help. Mom had been caring for Dad so much that she had neglected herself. She had sacrificed her own health, friendships, and self-care to manage his health and keep him safe. My brother was working either internationally or interstate and supporting us the best he could, though from a distance. I was trying hard to support Mom, but my work was demanding, and my young family was too. To make matters worse, Dane's mental health was heading into severe decline, and, at that point, no one knew about it. I was the glue that was keeping everyone together, yet my personal and home life was in significant disarray. I could see that our family structure was crumbling as it tried to stay afloat. Big time. Understatement.

We quickly put even more measures in place, onboarding carers and helpers. We stretched our financial resources to the maximum to help Dad receive the best care and ensure Mom was supported. At the same time, I was trying to support my husband and keep him alive while raising our two boys.

It was a few months into our new routine when I got a call from Mom and heard the words I'd never heard her say before. Her voice was empty and lifeless. "Nadine, I don't know how much longer I can go. I need a break," she murmured.

I knew this was her breaking point. Although we did have supplement carers in place (where we could afford it) and were doing everything else we could possibly do, she was at her maximum capacity and energetic output, and burnt out from carer's fatigue. So once again, we had to look at restructuring our care plan.

We already had aid with family government resources and aged care support, but we now needed to maximize Dad's care and heavily rely on some additional government support. We were scraping the barrel. Because he desperately wanted to stay at home, we had provided care in the home to meet his wishes. But now Mom was paying the price, and, to be honest, so was I and the rest of the family.

We had to face some harsh facts. Dad had nearly burnt down the kitchen twice. He got lost in the garage numerous times and couldn't remember where he was. We had the police turn up when Dad had secretly taken the car keys and headed out for a drive. When they found him, he couldn't tell them where "home" was. Dad couldn't be left alone, and Mom's around-the-clock care (even with some respite) wasn't working anymore. I was flying in and out to give Mom respite, but we were all going down like a sinking ship. We realized that Dad's care needed another major overhaul. Urgently!

I sent Mom away for some rest and relaxation while I pondered our next steps and contacted my brother to mull things over. Dad wasn't remembering much at all, yet he always remembered Mom and me. We were his only constant remembrance, especially Mom—he wouldn't take his eyes off her. Even through his decline, his eyes always searched for her, and his face eased whenever he saw her. In many ways, Dad was like a child; his illness revealed an innocence and vulnerability we rarely saw before he got sick. The cruel disease was ripping his mind to shreds but strangely, in his last years, also revealing the true softness of his heart.

He had many moments of beautiful lucidity—almost like the clouds of Alzheimer's parted and Dad appeared as we knew him. During these moments, he would often say things like, "Nadine, what are you doing here? Go back home and look after the kids." Or, "I'm so sorry you have to look after me. I never wanted it to be this way." He was so alert during these moments that I dropped whatever I was doing to just be present with him, to look into his eyes and soak up the preciousness of his clarity and spirit.

I gripped these tender moments like precious jewels. I knew

it could be mere minutes or even seconds before the haze of dementia would invade his mind and he'd be lost again behind the clouds of the disease. These tiny windows of lucidity were sacred gifts among the turmoil of caregiving. I held them in the vault of my heart and sometimes returned to them for comfort. To this day, I know these pockets of precious time with Dad were often what kept me going.

## A Broken System with Angels

Paradoxically, I was looking after Dad and my side of the family while my own family unit was barely hanging on. Dane's dad was very ill, and his mom was looking after him. I was severely torn and kept having bad visions of finding Dane lifeless from suicide when I got home. It was haunting me. The daily juggle was something I'll always remember. Between taking care of Dad and ringing my husband to make sure his mental health was at least survivable, I was swinging dangerously between being a nervous wreck and a fierce mother tigress. I nurtured the fierce energy flowing through me, as I often walked a thin line between breaking down and breaking through. I didn't know which would win: the breakdown or the breakthrough.

I was heavily involved in Dad's care from the beginning, and, with my nursing background, I was lucky to be able to navigate good care for him and talk candidly about his care with the medical staff. Dad's complex health issues meant his medical history was a mile long and he needed a special type of care. Leukemia, dementia, stroke, wheelchair-bound, with an aortic aneurysm, wasn't your average combination. Not to mention Dad's undiagnosed mental health issues that led him to depression and decades of alcohol abuse, a coping mechanism that was passed down generations upon generations, to suppress his trauma.

I met so many Earth angels on this journey. Medical staff so willing to passionately care for a mixed-up man without compromising his dignity. Yet being involved in his care also revealed how incredibly flawed our aged-care system is. I cried many tears thinking about all the aging men and women lost in the bureaucracy of government funding, poor treatment, and our lack of advocacy for them. I saw the best and worst of our system and fought tirelessly for Dad's best care. Navigating a flawed system is challenging. Sadly, it's a crisis in our country. A 2021 Royal Commission, along with eighteen major inquiries into aged care, confirmed that we are indeed in desperate need of change. Yet not much action has resulted. A government report says around 456,000 people rely on different types of care—residential care, home care, transition care, short-term restorative care—in Australia.[1] That's a huge number of people negatively affected by an inadequate system.

I have seen and spoken to so many families in crisis over caregiving. Beautiful people with big hearts trying to navigate a flawed system. I saw elderly people isolated and confused about their situation and their caregivers frustrated and exhausted. A shitshow where lives dangled precariously among a sea of paperwork, lack of resources, and undertrained and exhausted staff and caregivers just doing their damn best. Families like ours giving a fuck, and others giving ZERO. I saw it all.

Nothing can truly prepare you for being a caregiver. But I believe we can do a better job at making the system better for those who find themselves in that situation. And let's be honest—that's going to be most of us!

## A Stroke of Love

Because Mom was burnt out, I flew back home and told her, "Go out and have a day or two with your friends. Maybe also check in to a hotel and get a decent night's sleep. I've got things handled."

I was going to leave after a few days and head home to my own family, but Dad seemed a little off, and a little intuitive voice told me to stay. I worried about Dane being alone for too long, but something deep within told me to stay. I just pottered around, taking care of Dad, watching him like a hawk. He seemed to enjoy my company, and I was lucky enough to capture small glimpses of lucidity where I could see "Dad," the man I really knew. One evening, we just smiled at each other, and I told him how much I loved him. His eyes filled with beautiful tears of love, and we held each other's hands.

The next morning, I woke up and noticed he still seemed a little off. He said he had a pain in his hand. Then soon after that, he mentioned a metallic taste in his mouth and numbness and tingling. My stress levels hit the roof, and, as a registered nurse, I started checking for other signs. Within minutes, one side of his face was droopy, and he began to slur his words. I instantly knew he was likely having a stroke. I called an ambulance, and, after the assessment I gave over the phone, they were at our door within six minutes. His left side had become paralyzed, and he was vomiting from the intense pain and dizziness.

He had suffered a catastrophic stroke.

Dad was as tough as nails, and, despite his complex health issues, he wouldn't give up. His body was a mangled lopsided mess of skin and bones; he had lost the ability to eat and drink, and he was barely able to mutter a syllable. But underneath the medical monitoring tools and scurry of action, Dad was still drawing breath. Barely, but there was breath. He refused to die, and I love his stubborn streak (I think I inherited that from him).

It was the middle of the COVID pandemic, so dealing with the hospital policies and their "no contact" rules made it ultra-tricky, especially with someone suffering dementia. Using FaceTime to contact your sick loved one because the hospital says that's your only option feels so inhumane when all the person you care about needs is someone to hold their hand and stroke their hair. We did whatever we could to find ways around the rules while honoring the situation the staff found themselves thrust into. Whatever new rule the government enforced, we found a way to navigate it to support Dad. Often, that meant only one person could visit him per day and only for a limited time. But if we took him out for his designated 1-hour "outdoor time," we'd coincidentally "bump into" Mom in the park, and they would hold hands like teenagers. In these small moments, breaking the one-person government policy and social distancing rules was worth it. Seeing Dad's eyes light up was the most beautiful thing for a lost man in isolation who didn't even understand why we couldn't stay with him all day long. We took the opportunities we got and made the most of them. The hospital staff would often smile and say how beautiful it was to see a family so determined to see a loved one and find a way around the red tape!

After four months of hospital care and rehabilitation, Dad was discharged, wheelchair-bound and frail, but alive, and once again with a stoic family ready to love him until his last breath. This meant some major renovations to the house to accommodate Dad's new wheelchair, his shower chair, and other medical furniture and equipment. It was a huge emotional and financial commitment. We really didn't know how we were going to manage, but we were determined to look after him and honor his dignity.

Mom and Dad still lived in the same home I grew up in, and, although it probably should have been bulldozed at that point, it was "home" to us. We donned our overalls and did some of the world's quickest budget-friendly renovations to make the house workable with Dad's wheelchair. We bashed out bathroom walls and created space for his chair. We made ramps and stripped steps, magically turning them into flat surfaces. Dane built an entirely new veranda. We had concrete laid and surfaces rebuilt.

We didn't have the money to hire an assortment of tradies, so we just made do with what we had, Dane and me together like a scene out of *The Block* (me as his offsider). Fortunately, he was a carpenter in a former life. We literally made Dad's home livable and safe for him with our bare hands, and it was beautiful.

I remember stepping back and watching us laboring and sweating, all hands on deck, doing whatever we could to get Dad back home. It was at this moment that I thought, *Wow ... How much beauty there is in the shit fight. How much compassion there is in the struggle. How much care there is in the fight. How much love there is in the labor.*

I really saw the beauty in the fight. The messy moments that revealed the greatest love. How the ache of pain gave us gratitude for little moments.

## Leaning into Love

Dad never fully recovered from his stroke. Sure, he survived, but it was also a death sentence. We cared for him at home, this time with more medical issues and challenges to deal with than ever before. But I felt certain we'd find a way through it.

Dane and I juggled his mental health, bouts of depression, and PTS (post-traumatic stress), our young babies, and work, with our finances dwindling and both sides of our families experiencing huge challenges. Even though our relationship had taken a severe beating, we were teammates in crises, tag-teaming to cope. One would tap in, and the other would tap out. We'd alternate roles and just keep praying we'd make it through. I questioned the pillars of our relationship but couldn't give it my attention because we were too busy taking care of our parents. Our relationship was fraying, and Dane's mental health was like a ticking time bomb. Despite all this, I was focused on giving Dad and Mom the best while juggling the kids' needs and all my other responsibilities.

We spent lots of special family days together, ensuring the boys could spend quality time with their grandfather. I often told them stories about Dad so they'd be able to imagine what he was like before all of his chronic health problems. They would dote on him, and, among the dark times, we found ways to enjoy the moments we had.

As a family, we turned up the love dial to full pelt.

Luckily, I was sharing lots on social media, which made me feel better. I was honest and raw, and, in many ways, it acted as a kind of therapy for me. Strangers were often a beautiful comfort when I shared some hardships, and I felt a connection to so many complete strangers who were also battling similar hardships. The community was holding me emotionally, which created a special feeling among the duress. Sharing our journey was such a therapeutic outlet for me, and I was fortunate to have a community of beautiful and caring souls.

I really leaned on my community. Many strangers became friends, and they really got me through another day. I felt loved too, and I needed it. I had so many gorgeous people send me messages of hope, even beautiful flowers, freshly brewed coffees, and freshly picked bananas, which landed on my doorstep anonymously straight from the farm. I was blown away by the kindness of people.

As Dane and I were both navigating ourselves and our family and jumping in and out to care for Dad, some of God's angels swooped into our lives and became the bedrock of kindness and compassion we needed.

## The Invisible Toll

One thing I didn't notice was the toll caregiving was taking on me. After the stroke, Dad was having some major issues, and I was continually putting out spot fires to accommodate his decline. I was forfeiting sleep when Dad was restless at night. And because Mom was also so tired from taking care of Dad, we'd often suggest some sleeping pills to help her get at least some rest.

I remember one particular night when my sons Madden and Beckham were with me. Madden was only around six at the time, and Beckham was two. They were still very much dependent on me. Dad was waking up many times throughout the night wanting to go for a walk. Although he was wheelchair-bound most of the time, part of his dementia meant he often felt the need to pace. So he would climb over the bed rails (and they were freakin' massive rails too), fall onto the safety mat on the floor, and end up on the ground in an erratic state saying, "I need to go for a walk."

My back was aching that day, and the pain was adding another layer of agony to the situation. I had a toddler in bed sleeping, but Madden didn't want to sleep alone, so he was often up with me when Dad needed me. Not ideal.

This one night, Dad was up *thirteen times* needing to be outside. Yes, I was counting. I remember thinking to myself, *Fuck ... I can't do this anymore*. Dad wasn't well, and he was like a runaway train, simply adamant about being outside and pacing. He was a frightened man, not in his right mind, and the only way he felt he could get relief was to pace.

So there we were—Madden and me pushing Dad around outside in the cold in his wheelchair for the thirteenth time in the wee hours of the morning. I was depleted. Every part of me knew this entire scenario was a recipe for disaster.

Lo and behold, it started to rain. We got wet, and Dad was oblivious. I remember looking at Madden, outside on a wet night, his hair and clothes damp, as he tried to help me push Dad around. I thought, *What the fuck am I doing?* But we kept doing it anyway. To keep him dry, I gave Madden the layers I had on me, so when we finally got home, I was saturated. I dried everyone off and started yet another day of the grind, taking care of everyone else and leaving myself behind—because that's what good daughters and mothers do, right? Little did I know, I was about to receive a big wake-up call.

After a marathon of sleepless nights, I was driving home to reunite with my babies, and I nearly had a head-on collision with a truck on the freeway. Yep, you guessed it—it was my fatigue, my empty cup that nearly caused the incident. I nodded off for a split second and almost didn't wake up.

I pulled off to the side of the road, shaky. I stared at my

shocked pale-white expression in the rearview mirror. Tears welled. I had arrived at a point of danger. Serious danger. I spoke to myself in a way that held finality.

*Nadine, you cannot keep doing this. You're not superhuman. You've got kids who need you. You can't die. Not today. Not for a long time. You must change course NOW! This is killing you. This ISN'T what your dad, in his right mind, would ever want you to do!*

That was a turning point for me. I knew I would look after Dad as best as I could, but I would no longer ruin myself to do it, risking the lives of those around me too.

I was at capacity. I knew it was time. It was no longer safe for us, or Dad.

Although I had promised Dad that I would do whatever I could to keep him home, I simply could not keep that promise without breaking myself, Mom, Dane, Madden, and Beckham. It was time to make a tough call.

We were very fortunate that a beautiful lady, Karen, lived near us and had a nursing background, and we took her on as a private in-home support worker. Hiring private support after maxing out the other support available ran us financially dry. However, we were desperate and needed reprieve, so we did without many things and somehow just made it work.

Karen would arrive and relieve us of our grueling hours with Dad, helping us with his daily tasks. My gosh, I don't think we would have ever got as far as we did without her and the other beautiful private support workers who were part of our journey.

One particular day, Dad was feeling unwell, suffering from

multiple UTIs, and he seemed to be heading downhill. We knew we were losing the fight to keep him at home. I called Karen to get him ready, and I empowered Mom to make a decision for herself and Dad. It was, after all, their journey. Mom chose to call an ambulance, and we prepared Dad as best we could, physically and emotionally. I always wanted to keep him informed regardless of his mental state. He would need to spend some time in hospital, and we knew that this time it wouldn't be for just a few days. With Dad being unwell again and so many complications, we could no longer take care of him.

The staff at the hospital knew that our family's relentless mission to keep him home hadn't been half-hearted. Finally, I told them, "We've reached our limit. We all have carer's fatigue, and we can't look after his growing needs properly in the home anymore. It has become unsafe. We're desperate for help."

Of course, we needed to discuss his health and the possibility of him later entering an aged-care facility, among other things. But this time, instead of feeling swamped with guilt, I took charge. I rose up. I knew we were at the edge and if pushed further, we'd freefall. So I found my reason to rise, and that reason was the destiny of my family. I had to accept my edge. I had to acknowledge my capacity and honor it. I had to make the next hard decisions on behalf of my family—the one I knew no one else could make. Love is tricky like that, right?

Boundaries aren't easy to erect when you love people with all your heart and soul and you've promised to honor their dying wish. But sometimes promises and boundaries are about self-preservation and survival, and to ignore them is dangerous.

This was when I made the change from carer's fatigue to self-mastery. I had to acknowledge and accept when I had hit the brink. I had to silence my inbuilt conditioning to self-destruct in the name of "family honor." I was not going to be another tragic statistic in the family, and the collateral damage to my mom and my family was already too much.

Sometimes Mom would crumble and plead to bring him home again for a few days. It was so hard to say, "No, Mom, remember what we said. It's not safe anymore."

I spoke to the medical and social work team, telling them straight, "We can no longer safely provide Dad the care he needs, and the health of all of us is in a steep decline. We need help."

I didn't mention my near head-on collision with a truck, Dane's mental instability, or my kids' sleepless nights, but I did clearly tell them about Mom's carer's fatigue, and mine too. I simply and calmly said, "As much as this pains me deeply to say, he will no longer be able to be cared for in the home. It's as *hard* and as *simple* as that."

In that moment, I felt vindicated. I knew in my heart of hearts it was the right decision. It certainly wasn't the easy decision. It was a shit decision to have to make. But it is the harsh reality of caregiving, and we must rise to this reality and face the circumstances we're thrust into.

## Champions of Caring

If you're a caregiver, then you are a freakin' resilient badass! You are the one leading with love. A champion of caring! A changemaker in people's lives. And let me just say ... I'm so proud and in awe of you. Because I know what it takes, and jeez ... it's a huge undertaking. A mammoth thing to do. Caregiving takes bucketloads of courage and resilience. Not to mention energy and love.

Even with all the arduous roles and challenging situations in my life, to this day caregiving was easily one of my biggest feats. It was one of the most demanding jobs and the hardest mentally, emotionally, energetically, and physically I've had the HONOR to endure. If you're a caregiver, I see you right now, and I feel the weight on your shoulders.

But hey, superhero ... please look after yourself in the process! You think you're handling it, until you're not. A recent study showed that critical care nurses had high levels of moral courage, compassion, and loving-kindness, and low levels of self-centeredness.[2] I believe that is equally true for all champions of caring. But remember—it's very common for such beautiful, empathetic, and kind people to get burnt out and suffer from carer's fatigue.

As Tia Walker says in her book *The Inspired Caregiver*: "Caregiving often calls us to lean into love we didn't know possible."

Ain't that the truth!

## The Empty Cups of Caregivers

Caregivers are silent superheroes. They overcome obstacles and battle the toughest and most grueling situations with compassion, kindness, and care. However, it's important to highlight the dangers associated with being ultra-empathetic, which I will now do.

### ~ Carer's Fatigue and Burnout

Carer's fatigue refers to a crisis when the physical, mental, and emotional toll of caring for someone reaches an extreme phase and the caregiver suffers exhaustion and burnout. Carer burnout is not the fault of the caregiver! It occurs from being in a state of chronic stress, and is very real and very common. Studies indicate that approximately 60 percent of caregivers experience symptoms of carer's burnout.[3]

The Cleveland Clinic says, "Burnout feels like a candle that ran out of a wick—it doesn't have what it needs to continue to provide light. It can occur when you don't get the help you need personally, as you devote all of your time and energy to helping someone else. It can also happen when you try to do more than you're able to, emotionally, physically or financially."[4]

### ~ Compassion Fatigue

Compassion fatigue is a form of emotional and physical stress and exhaustion that can affect people who have been exposed to other people's traumas. It often affects healthcare workers and caregivers. Compassion fatigue can reveal itself through many different symptoms, including exhaustion, feelings of caring too much or emotional numbing out, a preoccupation with the suffering of others, or detachment and lack of empathy due to burnout.[5]

Compassion fatigue is a serious problem that can affect a caregiver's mental health and ability to care for others. Informal caregivers especially have a high risk of compassion fatigue and caregiver burnout.[6]

> *"Compassion is supposed to be a positive action.*
> *If it feels like work, it is probably too much.*
> *It indicates that it is time for a break or to*
> *engage in more manageable acts of compassion."*[7]
> —DR. ERIC ZILLMER,
> Professor of Neuropsychology, Drexel University

## ∼ Mental Health Concerns

Depression and anxiety are the most common mental health issues in the world and have been cited as the most frequent consequences of caregiving.[8]

Because caregivers are required to deal with heavy emotional loads under pressure, stressful decisions, and physical exhaustion, they are more likely to experience depression and anxiety. According to research, when a person has dementia or a neurodegenerative disease, the caregiver providing support is much more likely to experience depression and anxiety than adults of the same age not involved in caregiving.[9]

Caregivers are not only more likely to experience depression and anxiety, but they also report higher levels of stress and negative emotions such as guilt, sadness, and worry, along with regular feelings of isolation and grief.

## ∾ Physical Health Concerns

The mind and body aren't separate. We know that what affects one affects the other. Caregivers also battle the physical aspects of their role and are susceptible to fatigue, sleep disturbances, lower immune systems, dysregulated hormones, risk of injury or mortality associated with their responsibilities, higher use of health services and medication, and difficulty with cognitive function and memory.

Exhaustion and adrenal burnout are common among caregivers, and the sad truth is, over time, your "normal" becomes exhaustion, and you can't remember what optimal health feels like.

## ∾ Knock-On Effects

Of course, the mental, emotional, and physical issues are common, but there are also the secondary knock-on effects of being a caregiver, including:

- **Work stresses**—such as trying to communicate with a boss who "doesn't get it," or a reduction in hours and the financial strain associated with a change of circumstances, while trying to juggle all the responsibilities at once.

- **Financial pressures**—trying to pay for medical and health equipment and services that aren't subsidized while also trying to pay bills, for food, and all other associated expenses.
- **Paperwork and bureaucracy**—the paperwork and bureaucracy associated with dealing with hospitals, aged care, and an assortment of clinicians is endless and often frustrating. This adds additional pressure to an already stressful situation. Meeting eligibility criteria, getting funding, finding respite, dealing with technology and forms, and getting the right services in place can be a long waiting game, adding another layer of pressure and stress.
- **Relationship pressures**—the loss of time with partners, family members, and friends can really take a toll. Relationships are often strained when pressure at home changes your "normal" way of life. A difference of opinion between family members about the type of care or health decisions of a sick loved one can trigger deep emotions and add further relationship stresses.
- **Care decisions**—trying to make the right decisions for your loved ones is emotionally grueling. Deciding the type of care required and the level of support isn't always easy and often needs reviewing. Supporting the needs and wishes of your loved one while ensuring caregivers don't burn out or suffer too is a tremendous balancing act. These care decisions are hard and take an emotional and

mental toll. Discussing tough topics like medical risks, residential placement, and palliative care, carries a heavy load—that's why it's critical that caregivers have support.

## Coping or Crisis?

During the caregiving phase, it can be hard to figure out if you are actually coping or not. Adrenaline can fuel sleepless nights, and our fight-or-flight response has us equipped for most short-term crises. But caregiving isn't always short-term; often, it's one long marathon of medical interventions and caregiving support. This is why having a guide can be helpful.

I went through many different phases of caregiving, but because I was hell-bent on keeping Dad at home and honoring his wishes, I didn't see the massive "red flag" of crisis until I nearly hit a truck head-on. I suggest you find out earlier than I did. Much smarter (and safer) than coming eye to eye with an XXL Kenworth's bull bar. Anyway, knowing where you are on the scale between coping or crisis is really important in ensuring your health and wellbeing.

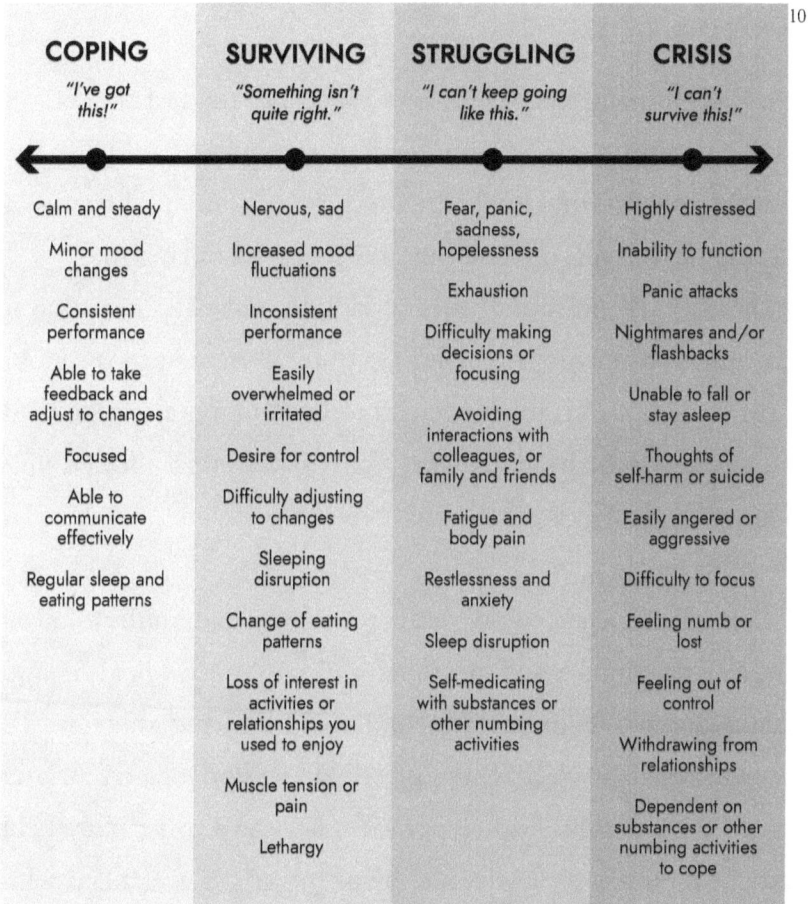

## Lucid Moments of Love

As I've mentioned, throughout Dad's battle with dementia, there were times when we got to see his "real self" shine through the foggy haze of his disease. He would have tiny sparks of lucidity, and we could see his true personality once again. I'd capture those moments in my memory banks, hanging on to the remnants of Dad when they appeared.

Although, throughout my life, Dad wasn't one for saying, "I love you," during his illness, and especially toward the end of his life, he would say it easily. There was so much healing in the final stages of his life that I can attest to the profound benefits of making peace with the hell that has occurred during life.

Dad became a man of such profound and deep love that it was quite extraordinary. The past trauma seemed to ooze out of his body, and his mind seemed to have found a way to deal with the demons. In many ways, maybe dementia allowed him to forget so many traumatic memories and return to the love he felt in his heart.

In his final days, I could clearly see that he had finally allowed himself, his younger self, his inner child, to receive healing and be love-bombed with pure, unconditional love and affection. To be seen, held, loved, and supported. He was advocated for and upheld with dignity and respect. Yet he was also lovingly held and caressed like a newborn baby as his bright eyes filled with so much innocence and peace.

During the cruel decline of his disease, we saw what love really looks like. We saw what devotion really means, and what unconditional love stands for. I wish I could have taken that disease from his tormented mind, but I am so grateful for the love that emerged from this harrowing experience. We healed the intergenerational trauma that bound him, and we didn't cycle it through to my children and beyond. We were the love medicine, the healing balm our lineage had been waiting generations upon generations for.

## The Long Walk Home

Fortunately and unfortunately, I've seen a lot of people die—young, old, in varied ways, peacefully, catastrophically, you name it, I've just about seen it all. However, holding my dad's hand while he moved from this life to the next took all my personal and professional resources. We created an environment that let him take his long walk home with love, care, and compassion.

Caregiving is love in action, and that's what our family displayed.

At the end, Dad looked like a prisoner of war, all skin and bones, but in a loving warm environment full of dignity and peace. As he started to make his transition from one life to the next, and as his morphine driver continued to increase in dosage, his consciousness slowly faded. As his daughter and the advocate for his care, I left no stone unturned, from the moment we decided to care for him in the home, through to when we laid him to rest and beyond. In those final days and hours, he was never alone—our family never left his side. We would sit in quiet honorable stillness; we would play his favorite tunes; we even watched him miraculously lip-sync the lyrics of his and Mom's wedding song when we played it in the room. That was a moment I'll always remember.

We chose to be in vigil. As a family who endured so much to arrive where we were, we would continue to walk this path graciously together. We ordered our local family pizza, bought some red wine, and were simply together as a family, soaking in the final moments, the last we'd all be together in this lifetime. My brother brought in some of our precious family heirlooms, which meant a lot to Dad and our family. Our beloved aunty and our boys came in to show their love for Dad and say their goodbyes, as we knew he was heading into his final days and hours. We held his hand, never leaving his side. We would caress his face and hair, share happy memories, and tell him over and over again how much we loved him. We thanked him for who he was as a father, husband, grandfather, friend, and sovereign being. We played Scottish bagpipe music and discussed our incredible Scottish lineage and the stories of our dear old dad we would continue to pass down.

The walls of his private room in the aged care facility were decorated with his grandchildren's paintings and mementos from home. His room resembled a family home more than a nursing home.

I ensured our boys came in to share "special time" with their grandfather, who they called "Grandpa." Dane and I knew that modeling a way to grieve and love was paramount, and we took our time together as a family, sharing special memories and loving on Dad in every way possible. We knew this would also support our boys in their continued life journey, especially with the cycle of life and losing those they love along the way.

Madden and Beckham talked about their happy and funny moments with Dad. They also told me later that when grandpa died, they wanted him to come back to them as a magpie. They were already thinking of him transitioning, and we made it beautiful instead of scary.

Mom organized the local Catholic parish priest to come and pray over Dad with end-of-life blessings and prayer. Although Dad wasn't exactly a churchgoing man, he was Catholic and found comfort in prayer and the idea of heaven. Mom, on the other hand, was devout and strong in her faith.

We told Dad how much we loved him all the way till his last breath and beyond. His eyes had a crystal-like clarity that I had never seen before and will never forget. His ocean-blue eyes sparkled, and the whites of his eyes were like pure white snow. Helping Dad feel at peace with the dying process was a huge privilege. I was holding his beautiful head, stroking his hair, and watching his chest fall slowly up and down with his breathing.

Over time, his breathing became slower and slower and grew shallower. I knew he was preparing to leave. I was in an elevated state of divine love and connection, and I could feel the bridge between heaven and Earth with an extreme and beautiful sensitivity. It was simply extraordinary. I could feel his soul preparing to leave, and I could intuitively sense when he was going to take his final breath. It was a surreal and incredibly intimate experience.

Mom was holding his hand when he took a big long sigh. She thought it was his last breath, but I intuitively knew it wasn't. I quietly said, "He's got another one." Then I repeated, "Keep walking, Dad. Keep walking." About a minute and a half later, he took his last breath, surrounded by his loving family. I held him close, and we all guided him with such grace and love as he made his walk from his human experience on Earth to heaven.

We stayed with him as his soul left his body. We didn't rush the process, and we held him with such love and devotion afterward too. He wasn't alone on either side of the veil. We loved him on Earth and in heaven with a fierce beauty that was undeniable.

Life and death hold such extreme dichotomies. They can be so brutal and so beautiful at the same time. The love we have shared becomes the grief that both sustains and breaks us.

Ensuring the process of Dad's death was sacred and intimate really helped our family say goodbye in the way we wanted. Not everyone gets that privilege. I feel very grateful and privileged that we got to say goodbye in a way that engulfed us and Dad in so much love and healing.

Of course, we cried bucketloads of tears and grieved our hearts out. But we also loved so deeply! And that's what I'm most proud of. I got to see and experience my dad's transformation before my eyes. I got to witness the profound effects of forgiveness, healing, and unconditional love. I got to see the journey of a dedicated marriage between my parents and how, after many ups and downs, they found peace, forgiveness, and an immense love that knew no bounds.

Death often leaves us with a renewed sense of gratitude for life and with an appreciation of the times we shared together. For some people, it can mean regret. Luckily for us, Dad's ability to open his heart and finally express love healed him of any potential regret.

It seems a bit odd to say Dad had a "good death," but if love was the indicator, then it was more than good. It was phenomenal.

## Caregiving as a Recurring Event

Of course, caring for Dad wasn't the only type of caregiving I was used to. As a wife and mother, I'm used to part of my identity being the role of caregiver. What has been harder, however, has been applying caregiving to myself. When I have been in hospital or suffering from an emotional trauma, giving myself love and allowing others to love and help me has been something I've had to learn to do. To be quite frank, I wasn't the quickest learner. I was hell-bent on appearing stoic and strong, even when I was in knee-buckling pain.

I have spoken to a lot of women who have also found this to be their Achilles heel. Why is it so much easier to love, support, and care for other people than it is to apply that same devotion and care to ourselves?

I've seen women who aren't supposed to walk after major surgery drive to the service station, hobble in on crutches, strain to pick up a carton of milk, and pray their stitches don't burst, all so their kids have milk for their breakfast cereal in the morning. Most women would nod, understanding that we ALL do batshit crazy things instead of asking for help.

I guess, historically, there has been an embedded (and often unspoken) culture that says looking after ourselves is selfish, and "good" mothers/wives/women/friends/daughters *should* sacrifice themselves for those they love and suffer in silence rather than speak their needs out loud.

Now, of course, we could get gung ho and blame society, the patriarchy, our innate ability to "rescue" others, and the subconscious saboteurs lurking in our psyches, and all would hold their own valid arguments. Though, of course, if we want to RISE and get radically responsible for the shit we create, then we must CHOOSE the life we want.

A quote often misattributed to Ernest Hemingway perfectly explains the potential pitfalls of love and caregiving: "The most painful thing is losing yourself in the process of loving someone too much and forgetting that you are special too."

Yes! We must validate, respect, and care for ourselves as we would others. Until we decide to do that, nothing will change, and we will remain victims within our self-made prison.

Therefore, I'm advocating for all caregivers to rise up, speak up, and stand up for yourself as you do others. You are someone special too. You deserve care too. You deserve nurturing too. It's time we stop the self-neglect and begin radical self-care.

## Radical Self-Care and Community Care

Looking after yourself is not selfish; it's smart. Sustainable caregiving can only work if self-care is part of the framework. Without it, I can almost guarantee someone will burn out and break down. That's why I'm calling it *radical* self-care—because when you're caring for someone you love and adore, the last thing you think about is taking care of yourself. It takes a radical act to think about your own wellbeing too.

One of my clients, Clare, found the idea grating indeed. She looked flabbergasted when I mentioned self-care, and said, "How can I think of myself when my husband is having multiple rounds of chemo and barely surviving?"

She had a point. How can we possibly think of ourselves when the person we love is in pain, or dying? The thing is, we don't need to *think*; we need to ensure our *behavior* supports our wellbeing. If we take care of ourselves, it ensures that we can keep taking care of the person we love in the best possible way. It's the good ol' "put your oxygen mask on first" analogy. And yes, it's counterintuitive to what we feel like doing. We love them so much that we want to give them everything we have. But here's the thing: *they* love *us* so much that they want us to be well.

Here are some simple tips to engage in radical self-care (the ideas aren't even that radical, but doing them … well, that's badass right there).

- Carve out time regularly to engage in activities you enjoy.
- Meet friends for a coffee or a walk and talk.
- Reduce exposure to additional stress wherever you can (or better yet, get others to do it for you).
- Erect boundaries that support your happiness and wellbeing.
- Exercise and eat well.
- Sleep, sleep, and sleep some more.

- Let people help you, hire people to help you (read that sentence again ...).
- Join a support group so you can chat with like-minded people.

I can honestly say that sharing my hardships and challenges on social media was my therapy. The community surrounded me with such love and care that I will never forget it, and I will forever be grateful. Strangers became friends, and some of the kindest people in existence stepped up to offer help when I could barely help myself.

**What I realized was this: what helped me and healed me more than self-care was community care.**

The collective love and support I received from my community did more than any mental health day, massage, or time at the beautician or gym ever could. Now I'm not saying those things aren't great—because they fucking are—but I am saying that community care was another layer of medicine. The love and care from others carried me further and higher than the self-care I could give myself.

> *"As you grow older, you will discover that you have two hands, one for helping yourself, the other for helping others."*
> —AUDREY HEPBURN

## Radical Gratitude

It's absolutely OK to make the shittiest time of your life the funniest. Or the most challenging time of your life the most radically grateful. Often, I would ask myself, *How can I make this ordinary circumstance extraordinary? How can I increase the peace in this challenging time? How can I increase my field of love?*

I found that looking for small things to be grateful for helped me enjoy the shitty times. For example, if a nurse brought me a cup of tea while I was bedside with my family, I would sip it with such reverence and thankfulness. It was a moment of peace among the turmoil.

Throughout my experience, I found that being grateful for the small things helped me cope with the big-ass challenging things. Love bombing Dad helped us soothe the ache in our hearts. Being grateful for the time we had together helped us appreciate the fact that we got to say goodbye.

Going through extreme back-to-back shitstorms helped me find what I value and love. I discovered what's worth RISING for and what's worth letting go of. I found my depth of compassion, and I also found my edge. I found a way to erect boundaries when I needed to, and I found that my "hustle and grind" mentality has its limitations.

Using gratitude to empower yourself is important. Don't use gratitude to make yourself feel worse. That's not a healthy practice—it's toxic.

Finding gratitude and peace among shitstorms helps, but it doesn't solve the situation. You will still need to get up and do what you must, but finding sprinkles of fun and laughter along the way is important.

We found the tiniest ways to smile among the hellish times. We found that gratefulness grounded our expectations and helped us feel appreciation for what we were enduring as opposed to merely wishing it was another way.

 Scan the QR code for your gratitude resource from my heart to yours.

# Gratefulness Exercise

*What are you grateful for?*

...........................................................................................................................

...........................................................................................................................

...........................................................................................................................

...........................................................................................................................

...........................................................................................................................

...........................................................................................................................

...........................................................................................................................

...........................................................................................................................

*Who are you grateful for?*

...........................................................................................................................

...........................................................................................................................

...........................................................................................................................

...........................................................................................................................

...........................................................................................................................

...........................................................................................................................

...........................................................................................................................

...........................................................................................................................

*Did a specific crisis or shitstorm give you something important? Or did it help you recognize what you value?*

*What traits do you have that you're grateful for?*

........................................................................................................................................
........................................................................................................................................
........................................................................................................................................
........................................................................................................................................
........................................................................................................................................
........................................................................................................................................
........................................................................................................................................
........................................................................................................................................
........................................................................................................................................

*What little things help you feel grateful?*

........................................................................................................................................
........................................................................................................................................
........................................................................................................................................
........................................................................................................................................
........................................................................................................................................
........................................................................................................................................
........................................................................................................................................
........................................................................................................................................
........................................................................................................................................

"Faith is the bird that feels the light and sings when the dawn is still dark."

—RABINDRANATH TAGORE

CHAPTER 8

# THE NEXT EVOLUTION

There is a future that awaits everyone, a glorious future that enables you to bathe in the best that life can offer. As you would understand from reading this book, your best life doesn't get handed to you on a silver platter. Though, once you draw on the infinite resources and decide to rise, and rise again, dormant forces awaken within you and bring out your internal compass, qualities, skills, and invaluable opportunities to direct your destiny.

Although society often wants you to learn cookie-cutter approaches and join systems that offer a "one-size-fits-all" policy or procedure to follow, you don't have to do what everyone else says you *should* do, or what society suggests is "standard" or "common."

You know in your heart what is best. Your internal guidance system—your intuition and mind-heart coherence—is yours to use, and it has a wisdom that is built for you specifically. You have an innate ability to discern what is right for you, and it doesn't have to be what everyone says is right for you.

You don't have to be "normal." In fact, I suggest you don't be. Be yourself and harness your inbuilt uniqueness. Because it's that uniqueness you will offer the world, and it's that original and "one-off" human we need. There is no one in the world like you. You are a complete original masterpiece. Therefore, you don't need to be guided by cookie-cutter approaches or fit neatly into the box that others suggest you belong in. You don't belong in a box at all. You are here to shine your magnificence in all its glory.

If I had listened to others, I'd still be in the military and still on dreaded back-to-back night shifts as a nurse. I'd still be working the inflexible hours dictated by others and working in the way they demanded. Although there is nothing wrong with that, it wasn't *my* way to stay. It wasn't my path long term. There was more, much more for me in my future.

It takes risk and courage to listen to your soul and follow its direction. It takes a whole lot of grit to navigate life in a way that doesn't conform to typical rules and regulations. There are other ways to be. You can still obey the laws of life without compromising your dreams.

Of course, as I've said before, it's not one long journey in paradise where nothing goes wrong, but it's certainly *your* journey, defined by your choices, goals, and dreams.

There is a new evolution awaiting you ... and it's the unfolding of your highest self. It's the transformation you've been waiting for. It's what will quench your soul and ignite your passion and purpose.

And it's waiting for you to claim it. Remember, at the start of this book, I suggested that making a decision to rise is one of the best decisions you can make. Well ... if you haven't already made that decision, here's your moment. Will you rise? Or will you stay right where you are and never know the thrill of rising? The choice is yours.

## It Wasn't Meant to End Like This

I now need to share something deeply intimate with you. This is not the ending chapter I had planned. I planned a full-on happy ending. You know the one—where we all live happily ever after, and nothing ever goes wrong again. Unfortunately, the ending we want isn't always the ending we get.

In January of 2024, I fell pregnant, and it was an incredible surprise. Dane and I had just decided to add "just one more" to our family and—boom! It happened during the first ovulation cycle. I didn't see it coming, and Dane and I were equally shocked (in the greatest way possible!). After so much drama from my last two pregnancies, I wasn't expecting it to happen so fast. However, a precious little one had decided it was time to immediately nestle in my womb and start its journey, and we were all beyond thrilled, especially our two boys who were excited to become big brothers. During a visit to Dad's resting place, I shared the news with Mom, and she cried tears of joy. It was a special moment.

Given my experience with my previous pregnancies, I figured it wouldn't be long before I was feeling rough again, so we decided to tell family and close friends very early. However, I held the projection that with all the deep healing and work I had committed to over the years the pattern wouldn't repeat. I remained in trust and detached from what this journey would be, surrendering to my path.

Of course, simultaneously we were in our high-tempo season of the year, conducting our transformational retreats (four retreats and two events and workshops back-to-back), so, the days were long and arduous, even when performing in optimal health and peak energy states. This round of retreats was yet again another raving success, and I managed to run them while pregnant, even though, at times during that first trimester, exhaustion and fatigue set in. I took the time where needed, resting every spare moment I could, and both Dane and I were so beautifully surprised at how great my mind and body was during this pregnancy. While it wasn't a walk in the park, finally I had a pregnancy where I could function—a HUGE win.

We spoke deeply about all the generational work and healing I had done in my lineage, which included an incredibly unwell mother line. I was the one to heal that repeating story in our mother line, and the overwhelming sense of personal pride, purpose, and how powerful the healing, growth, and generational repatterning work had been was just another reminder of my achievement.

After the retreats, and given the difference in this pregnancy, we went back on the road, resuming van life as a family of four, with another one on the way. I checked in with the obstetrics team just before heading across the country to Western Australia to make sure everything was OK with me and bubs. The doctor gave us the green light to travel and said that everything was looking great and to enjoy the travels ahead!

I'm sure you can imagine—I was so surprised on the daily that I wasn't vomiting every two seconds, hooked up to an IV line, or in hospital like I was with my previous pregnancies. I even had a distinct glow about me, and, at times, a spring in my step. It was like chalk and cheese. This may sound strange, and perhaps other HG (hyperemesis gravidarum) women can relate, but I often found myself worrying that if I wasn't sick enough, something was wrong. However, regular routine medical check-ups and tests reassured us that everything was progressing smoothly. Finally, a pregnancy I could enjoy! Now, don't get me wrong, I still had bouts of sickness. I still had days in bed with fatigue and exhaustion, though it was a far cry from my previous pregnancy experiences.

We were heading to the outback and rural outskirts, so we planned the next leg of the trip meticulously, ensuring access to ongoing care and routine doctor checkups and scans, just like normal, with our team taking care of us remotely along the way. With access to healthcare, technology, and an amazing dedicated team, everything was progressing perfectly.

The wide open roads, the red dust, and the sheer beauty and vastness of our great country always grounds and energizes me in a way I can't explain. Plus, I was relishing every moment of togetherness and time with my family—Dane, the boys, and my new growing baby. I kept thinking about the incredible story of my life. *How lucky am I?* But it was more than just luck. I was living a life I had bravely created by having the courage to go after it!

I still carried this nagging feeling of "not being sick enough," but I didn't want to play that old story through my mind. This time, baby was a girl, which might explain the different experience. Perhaps I was just running old narratives and programs, reliving past traumas and fears. I knew the power of telling myself a new story, so that's what I did. I reminded myself of new evidence that I knew to be true: *Women all around the world are well all the time throughout their pregnancies (heck some women feel their very best when they're pregnant!), so I can be well too.* It didn't have to be the way it had been previously; it could be different. I kept reminding myself that I could, and that I get to, enjoy this pregnancy. My past doesn't define my future.

Despite our best planning, getting seen by rural doctors wasn't always easy. Some appointments would be postponed due to staff shortages, problems with equipment, or technical issues. When we got to Geraldton, one of the bigger rural towns in WA, (about five hours' drive north of Perth), I wanted to ensure that bubs and I were still progressing beautifully. No matter what I told myself, I needed confirmation (again!) because this "well" feeling was so foreign to me.

I voiced my concerns to Dane, and, as usual, he was supportive and made sense of it all. He held the vision of everything being OK and allowed me room to feel whatever was emerging. We both knew that my fears around pregnancy and birth made sense and that having a different type of pregnancy was new mental and emotional territory for me. He held the perfect vision for us as a couple (which I needed him to do) while we waited for our next routine checkup and scan.

The obstetric sonographer got called away, so it would be a few days wait for the scan. But we weren't in a rush, and although we could have moved on to the next large town, something within me compelled me to stay.

"We'll wait for the appointment," I said. And we did.

## The Moment

The heat in Geraldton made me sweat more than usual, or maybe it was the thought of the upcoming scan. Finally, the time arrived, and Dane, Madden, Beckham, and I all trudged into the waiting area. The boys were excited to see bub on the screen, and I was too, though that feeling of uncertainty was still present.

The room was dimly lit, and the gel was cold and smooth. The sonographer made her usual movements, searching for the baby. Apparently, the baby was nestled away in an odd position.

Given my emergency nursing background, with the many

obstetric patients I'd seen come through those doors, I instantly knew the scan didn't look "normal." My heart sank. This was the moment I had feared. The moment I had heard other women discuss but hadn't experienced myself. Until now.

The silence in the room grew thick, and the sonographer's eyes were zoned in, investigating as she maneuvered around.

"I'll need a second opinion on this," she said. "Can you wait?"

I thought she meant wait a few minutes, maybe ten, but we in fact ended up waiting six hours for a second opinion of the scan. During this time, Dane and I had many deep and beautiful conversations. We both felt a deep need to connect and strengthen each other and the boys. Something in the scan wasn't right; my intuition was telling me a truth that I didn't want to face. I hadn't been told anything about the baby's fate yet, but I sensed that her destiny had already been decided.

Our second opinion came in the form of a tornado.

"Nadine, I am so sorry, we are transferring you right now, as you need to go to emergency straightaway. You will be prepared for emergency surgery today. I can confirm that your baby has no heartbeat and has passed in your womb, and there is a significant blood mass that has formed. Your blood count is severely critical. We are worried about a significant hemorrhage."

It felt like my heart had been ripped from my chest. Blood was collecting heavily in my womb and preparing to hemorrhage, and our choices were limited.

I was advised that the scan could only reveal so much, so the obstetric surgeon and team were running through all the scenarios and preparing for any and all circumstances. They could see the size of the mass and feared it rupturing. They knew something was deeply wrong, and so did I. Signing consent for a potential hysterectomy was not on the plan for what was meant to be a routine scan.

This was the moment I've heard so many of my clients talk and emotionally release about—the unpredictable loss of their baby, whether that be through miscarriage or other means.

I have held so many mourning mothers in my arms, and now that mother was me. I felt every woman whose story I have witnessed and whose pain I have compassionately held but never experienced, until now. I really felt them all with me. Their stories and mine intertwined like a woven tapestry of love and pain. We bled together in a way only mothers can know.

I had a new reality. My baby would not be born alive. The boys would not have their little Baby P (a cute little nickname our family gave her) to smooch and dote over. I had officially joined the grieving-moms club, a club no mother or parent ever wants to join, or should have to join.

While our situation wasn't unique, time was pressing, and the team were rushing to head into surgery quickly. Tapping in intuitively, I was divinely guided to reduce the pace a bit, and I asked for more time. Dane and I felt we needed to ensure the boys had some sacred space to grieve and ask questions. I knew it was a medical emergency, but it was also an emotional emergency, and one we had to navigate well, especially with little people involved who were just as shell-shocked as their mom and dad. How we chose to handle this grief experience for the boys imprinted what grief looks and feels like. We had time, so we took it. That's not to say I wasn't cognizant of the emergency, but I knew we didn't need to rush, so I advocated for a slower pace. Not just for the boys, but for me and Baby P too. After all, these were our final moments together, moments where both of us were together in-body. I was in a stable condition, under observation and receiving vital sign assessments every 15 minutes, and the team was on standby ready for surgery. I saw no reason to rush the process.

We explained the situation to the boys and held them as they said goodbye to their baby sister. They put their faces to my belly and said their Earthside goodbyes to their beloved sibling. They rubbed my belly and shared sacred words and prayers with her. We all embraced and hugged and cried and grieved the final moments we had together with Baby P. My embraces with Dane were truly something special. The true divinity of the divine masculine and the divine feminine. Two energetic souls standing before one another, having to say goodbye to our baby before we even had a chance to say a proper hello. Heartbreaking.

In our true family style, the boys beautifully asked Baby P if she could reveal herself and show up for them in the future so they knew she was there with them. Just like they asked Grandpa to appear as a magpie, they asked if Baby P could show up in special ways too. Baby lizards, geckos, and brown-yellow butterflies—so specific, right? Trust me when I say, just like magpies, these show up everywhere we go!

My surgery was expected to take no longer than 1 hour. However, not knowing exactly what to expect once they opened me up meant it could take longer. We said our painstakingly difficult yet necessary goodbyes to one another, and Dane left with the boys to support, guide, and debrief them at a nearby playground with some ice cream.

While all this had been happening, our 22-foot caravan and our tow vehicle were parked right out the front of the Geraldton Emergency Department, with our dog standing guard. It must have looked quite the sight!

Before the general anesthesia took over, I rubbed my belly for the last time with my beautiful baby, said my own personal goodbyes and prayers, told her I'd see her again soon, and took a deep breath.

## Far from Straightforward

Now to the surgery … and straightforward it was not. The "short" surgery soon turned into another unpredictable series of events. Dane received a phone call from the obstetrics specialist surgeon who had already consulted with other specialists at larger hospitals due to the intricacies and findings. The surgeon explained that they were experiencing some unforeseen discoveries and needed to have some deep and confronting discussions while I was under general anesthetic.

"While currently we've got control of the rupture, we have concerns and wish to gain your consent for a blood transfusion if she hemorrhages."

Dane was quick to remind them that we already gave consent for a blood transfusion and encouraged them to do it if necessary.

During the surgery, they discovered "abnormal cells" across my cervix and womb, which could lead to a recurrence of the cervical cancer scare in my twenties. While my cells had presented normally during routine Pap smears and specialist checks, the early signs of cancer had resurfaced but remained undetected—until now.

On the phone, the surgeon explained the situation to Dane. Along with removing baby, they would need to remove a fallopian tube and the blood mass and resect part of my womb, which would hugely affect my ability to have children in the future. GREAT! What a series of bombs to drop on Dane, all in one conversation, while I'm still under general and he is unable to consult with me.

Luckily, during our 6-hour wait for a second opinion, and with my intuitive sense of impending doom, Dane and I discussed a lot. We talked about our baby, my health choices, and the idea of extending our family, or not. We were fully together with our thoughts and entertained countless hypothetical situations. Although Dane didn't want another traumatic situation, with me undergoing yet another surgery with yet another baby, he knew which decisions were important to us. He knew what mattered to us as a couple and a family. This was the first surgery since the traumatic event of Beckham's birth, and Dane was once again thrust into the position of having his wife and child undergo a life-changing, and perhaps life-threatening, operation.

The doctor said it would be beneficial if we allowed him to make decisions while I was on the operating table. Otherwise, they might need to stop the surgery and go back in another time. It would mean one surgery potentially becoming several. Dane gave the instruction to do whatever was required, with the hope, but not expectation, of saving as much of my womb as possible. He also instructed them to do whatever necessary to save my life over saving my reproductive organs—there was to be no unnecessary risk to my safety. Dane knew that we would face whatever challenges arose together, even if it meant not having another baby. Above all else, I needed to live to be a mother to our boys.

Under anesthetic, I had another wild (and I mean wild) experience. My soul went "somewhere," and I vividly recall spending time with Dad and meeting Baby. I got to experience the gift of Dad's love and his warmth surrounding her. I intuitively knew he was receiving her now and would take care of her. She was so beautiful, angelic. She had this white light to her and a healing energy that I carry with me forever. Dad was a younger version of himself, so happy, healed, free of dementia and health ailments, and it was so beautiful to reconnect and see him in this way. I was given insight into the gift of Baby being here, why her short life was destined, and what her role on Earth was for our family. The love she has for us is so big. She couldn't join us because sacrificing a life was necessary to keep us together. She knew she would be with us anyway, just not in the way we thought.

Some things just cannot be described in words. My spiritual experiences, transcendence, and journeys continue to both surprise and ground me. I can't unsee what I know to be true now. The veil is thin. Both for me and my personal experience, and the experiences we get to lead, guide, and support in others too. Being in this "other world" is unspeakable in many ways. But for some reason, my most traumatic moments have come with the gift of a deep trove of spiritual treasures and wisdoms, and the deeper understanding of why things are the way they are. I really wish I didn't need full-blown near-death experiences and surgeries to have these moments of realization, but that's how it has played out for me so far.

Finally, at the end of the surgery, Baby P took her journey "home." In many ways, I had what felt like hours with her and hours with Dad. I was happy and grateful for that precious time. As I came out of the surgery, my mind was filled with this anchored memory. I felt blessed and full of love for Dad and Baby P, who were now taking great care of one another until we would all meet again. How lucky to know they are together. Not just wish, but really know.

I was still very groggy after surgery, and, as I came to, I could see that the time was 10 p.m. I had gone into surgery at 2 p.m. ... so not the 1-hour surgery originally expected. I noticed the size of the gauges in both arms—they were the type used for blood transfusions. Yet again, another nonlinear non-straightforward experience. The type of experience I've come to know very well in my lifetime.

My recovery room was in the maternity ward, and my heart instantly went out to all the women who had woken up the same way ... in the maternity ward, surrounded by the sound of women birthing and babies crying. In a room that still held a change table and a baby bath. An empty room, with an empty cot, and a heart full of pain.

I thought, *They should remove those items.* Women should not wake up from surgery, a D&C, a harrowing still-born birth, or a catastrophic event surrounded by baby items, yet no baby. Luckily for me, I was gifted the deep realization of knowing that my angel baby was safe and well and that my dad was with her. Others likely didn't have that experience.

Dane and the boys came in and covered me with warmth and love. The situation was beautiful. The boys were loving on me in a way that made me proud of the young men emerging inside them. I was totally surrendered and couldn't care for myself, so they jumped into action and took it upon themselves to care for me. I was mumbling about Grandpa and Baby P being together, saying we had a ginger beer together.

Dane was trying to fill my hazy mind with the details on what had occurred. I was starting to feel nauseous and ill from the general anesthetic, so my ability to comprehend the enormity of what had happened was limited. Instead, I basked in my family's love and tenderness and the knowing that life really is so finite. I smiled at how natural the play between the masculine and feminine energies was and how my young boys were stepping up and honoring me and their late sister too.

## A Gift from an Angel Baby

The surgeon arrived the next morning to discuss what had happened the day before. Her usual analytical and matter-of-fact tone was somewhat softer, with a touch of bewilderment. She told us she had only ever seen a case like ours once in her career, and she had been in obstetrics for nearly three decades.

She told me that if we had continued our outback trip, especially as we were heading into areas where emergency services would have taken hours to respond, the outcome could have been catastrophic. In the worst case, I would have needed medical attention within minutes. The blood mass could have, and likely would have, ruptured, and it was highly likely both Baby P and I would not have survived the hemorrhage. My gut instinct to stay in Geraldton was literally lifesaving.

On top of that, due to the requirement for surgery, the surgeon had detected the abnormal cells, which, if left untreated, had the potential to grow into something sinister, like cervical or ovarian cancer. In many ways, Baby P gave me a gift. She gave her life to save mine. She revealed where cells were forming and made damn sure the surgery brought them to light (in fact, Baby P had wrapped her tiny body around them). Because of her, they had to perform intricate surgery in the exact location where the cells were growing. I wholeheartedly believe she saved my life, and the doctors seemed just as gobsmacked as me. While the surgeon explained everything quite clinically, she couldn't deny the grace of the miracle.

In the months following the surgery, numerous people reached out to me. Even people who weren't in my tight circle messaged me. And they all said the same thing: our baby had appeared to them in a dream, and she always had a message to give. They all referred to "her," and they all felt compelled to reach out. The continual confirmation was beautiful.

Baby P continued to appear to people in dreams, and they would inevitably reach out. While Baby and I connect all the time, it was nice to have these connections from others too. She was beautifully guiding so many mamas who had also experienced loss. She continually reminds me that the veil between heaven and Earth is very thin and that love and connection extend beyond our mortal world.

After surgery, the surgeon had given me some strong advice about allowing my body time to repair. She said it could be a six-month or longer process and I needed to allow my womb to regenerate and repair itself. There was a missing cavity, a lost fallopian tube, and a massive part of my womb completely cut away. However, it is still possible I can have a child, even with parts missing. The surgeon reassured me that it could be done but only if I allowed adequate time for rebuilding and regeneration and continued my healing journey—mind, body, and soul.

Over time, people continued to reach out with messages from Baby P, and I knew what was coming next. Finally, several more people reached out, saying they needed to tell me something important but didn't want to upset me.

I knew this message well. I knew it so well because I was writing an entire damn book on the ability to RISE again. To be the phoenix from the ashes. To rebuild a life from the pits of despair. But not only was I writing about it, I was living it. Not just once, but again and again. I guess if you're going to preach an idea, God will make sure you're congruent with it through experience.

Well ... here it was yet again. Seriously??

Six months after losing Baby P, we experienced a second loss, a beautiful baby boy named Baby B. We lost him in the most heartbreaking way to a cornual pregnancy, which is quite rare (less than 1 percent of ectopic pregnancies). Of course, we were devastated, and once again we began the process of healing, with love and trust that baby number three would eventually join us Earthside. Until then, we would wait, for our double rainbow, always ready to face life's next set of challenges, always willing to rise again.

## A Reason to Rise

For this book, I really wanted the "and she lived happily ever after" finish. The Hollywood one where I'm holding the trophy and shouting for joy. But life doesn't always go that way. Although I've continually trained my mind and body to be resilient, life continues to challenge me and find ways to make me stronger, humbler, and more grateful.

In many ways, I'm a statistic, as one in five women in Australia have a miscarriage or lose a baby in pregnancy before twenty weeks.[1] Although Baby P was my first experience of losing a baby, and then next Baby B, I know and have held so many women who have cried uncontrollably while sharing their grief with me. I now understand that pain at a deeper level. I walk beside them. I am now one of those women who knows that pain.

I believe that Baby P and Baby B are my guardian angels. The fact that Baby P came for such a brief time and positioned her little body in the right place to raise the alarm saved my life. She gave her life for mine. Although some people may argue that I'm just searching for meaning in both of my tragedies, I would argue otherwise. Tragedy is fertile with meaning. Often, because of it, we love harder, become more grateful, more human, humbler, kinder, wiser, stronger, and softer all at once. We remember that we are connected. When my boys say "hello" to a little lizard, gecko, butterfly, or tiny chirping birds, I see a connection that transcends time and space and reminds us of what matters most—love and each other.

Now, of course, like any woman, I wish I didn't have to experience deep grief. But those are the cards we were dealt, and I am determined to never let grief or heartache become all of me. It's a part of me, but it's not all that I am. Both my angel babies will always be a part of me, and I will live in full love and gratitude because I was blessed to be their mom, even if for a short time. We are bonded for life, and they will stay with me and embrace all the women we laugh and cry with and love at every retreat.

I do not believe this is the end of my story, though I do believe it's a reason to RISE. A reason to rise again, to grow more, to understand others more than before, and to be grateful for life.

I will heal, and I will rise again. Rising isn't just a one-time deal. My life is a cycle of burning, finding strength among the ashes, and rising again. I believe this is what we all must do.

Do your best, embrace the rest, take a breath, and rise again.

It's not a question of *if* we will get burnt—adversity is an inevitable part of the human experience—it's how we walk through the fire that matters. How we rise from the ashes and soar with stronger wings. As ancient poet Rumi said, "A heart filled with love is like a phoenix that no cage can imprison."

So, who will you be in your next evolution of self? What new version of you is asking to burst from the cocoon and spread its wings? Sometimes we must let go of the person we once were and allow the next evolution to emerge.

The journey of rebirth, resurrection, and rising again isn't easy. In fact, it's guaranteed to be rough sailing. But know this—every time you rise, you do so stronger, wiser, more resilient than before, leaving behind the ashes of who you were to become the next iteration of your true and powerful self. What better reason to RISE?

# LET'S CONNECT!

Join our amazing community worldwide, online or face-to-face.
Is it time to create your dream life? Get ready to RISE!

Scan the QR code to review all of your
*A Reason to Rise* bonus tools and resources.

# TESTIMONIALS

"Nadine changed my life! I didn't even realize how much I needed her until I got started, and then it was wow, wow, wow. She introduced me to the person I was always meant to be but had lost along the way! I am happier, healthier, and giving my husband and kids the best version of myself. Forever grateful to have landed in her universe!"

— Brooke

"A weekend like no other! I can't express how grateful I am to Nadine, Dane, and the team, and how life-changing these experiences have been for me. I am free. I am lighter. I am happy. I am ME, and I am so freakin' proud of who I am!

"This work is unlike anything you have ever experienced or will ever experience; it's the unearthing of ALL the things, the surrendering of past stories, the energetics, the spiritual work, the unleashing of the masculinity mask, and the welcoming of *femininity attributes. It's the safest space to be, judgment-free ... It allowed me to go ALL in. I was committed, and it brought me HOME. I am freakin' HOME!"*

— Michelle

"We got to reclaim, reignite, and unite our love—for ourselves individually and as a couple! This weekend marked a fresh beginning for us on so many levels. Our connection is stronger, our love is deeper, and we are on a whole new level of togetherness. We get to experience and feel this transformation, and our children get to witness and feel it too.

"We have powerfully transformed! I can't thank Nadine, Dane, and the team enough for what we experienced—the unleashing of emotions, the challenges. We were supported every step of the way, which ultimately guided us onto the BEST path together. Thank you so much; we will be forever grateful!"

— Meghan & Craig

"Where do I even begin? The support and encouragement from Nadine are next level. The community she has created for women in similar situations and backgrounds is truly something you don't want to miss out on. I've met some amazing ladies, forming lifelong friendships in the process.

"Next on my list is the RISE retreat and EXPAND AND ELEVATE (three-month life and business mentorship), and to say I'm excited is an understatement. Being part of the Bloom *community is also incredible, as it provides constant support and encouragement right at your fingertips."*

— Jenelle


*"Working with Nadine is truly life-changing. She has opened doors to countless opportunities and immense personal and business growth for me. Nadine provides a space where I can express myself without judgment, and she cheers and supports me every step of the way. She is a true leader who embodies what she teaches. I highly recommend working with Nadine—she is the ultimate game changer!"*

— Libni


*"Yesssss! I seriously cannot believe what's happening and especially how my mindset has transformed! I appreciate you so much, Nadine. I just wish I had found you sooner. Thank you!!! Xxx"*

— Arra


*"Nadine is an epic human who goes above and beyond in every way. Her dedication, discipline, and the level of support she provides for her work, as well as the growth and trajectory change of humanity, are phenomenal and beautiful to witness and be a part of."*

— Davina

A REASON TO RISE

# ACKNOWLEDGMENTS

I am deeply grateful to my life accomplice Dane. There is nothing that together we cannot endure, overcome, and accomplish—my confidant, my muse, my love. Until the wheels come off, my one true love.

For my boys, Madden and Beckham. For rebirthing me over and over, for being my true North Star. You are the life coaches I never knew I needed. Thank you.

For my angel babies, Baby P and Baby B, until we meet again. Thank you for living out your mission and ultimately saving my life, thank you for guiding your brothers and protecting Daddy and me, and guiding our future double rainbow baby to bless us when the time is divinely right. In you, I have so much faith and belief in what's possible.

For my mom, brother Aaron, and my late dad, for your unwavering belief in and love for me. It's unmatched. We didn't have it all, though together we had all that actually mattered. To my aunt and uncle who I have been gifted as bonus parents my whole life, I am forever grateful for your undeniable support to Aaron and me.

To my Muller family, for welcoming me with open arms as your third daughter, your bonus sister, for the gift of your son, and the gift of birthing your grandchildren. I am so proud to pass down the Muller legacy.

To my mentors, spiritual teachers, and guides for your truths and transmissions that have served my mastery and my spirit. Thank you.

To the NMCM team, without each of you this global mission can't run as smoothly as it does. You are family, and I'm beyond blessed to have you right beside me.

Special thanks to editor Nat Deane and for her undeniable expertise and otherworldly wisdoms, not to mention the invaluable assistance of the entire family over at Dean Publishing and Simon & Schuster.

To the NMCM and Heartled Warrior family and clients to all the phenomenal humans I've had the pleasure, privilege, and honor to develop and lead, I might be the catalyst seen to be inspiring you, though thank you for each inspiring and showing me why my work matters so much for this world.

To the bravery of those who dare to make a difference with your leadership and intuitive gifts for the world. Keep sharing, keep using your voice, and keep enacting change. The world needs you!

For YOU the reader who finds a piece of yourself within these very chapters. I see you. Keep choosing courage over fear.

And finally, to the younger version of me, who chose to awaken and RISE. I am so proud of you. We did it x

# ABOUT THE AUTHOR

Nadine Muller is a high performance coach, life and business mentor, author, and multi-seven-figure entrepreneur who is on a mission to awaken people's gifts, unlock potential, accelerate growth, and help purpose-led people lead bold and wildly successful lives.

Her specialty is leading high-level and high-impact private mentorships, bespoke and exclusive group experiences, and high-caliber masterminds and workshops. She also leads healing and transformational retreats, and fiercely and unapologetically leads her clients to exponential growth, infinite freedom and wildfire abundance in all facets of their lives.

 Scan the QR code to visit nadinemuller.com.au, or connect on Instagram @nadinemuller.

# ENDNOTES

## Chapter 1
1. Murakami, Haruki. 2006. *Kafka on the Shore*. Vintage: New York.
2. Lichtman, Yael, Tamar Wainstock, Asnat Walfisch, and Eyal Sheiner. 2020. "The Significance of True Knot of the Umbilical Cord in Long-Term Offspring Neurological Health." *Journal of Clinical Medicine* 10, no. 1 (December): 123. doi.org/10.3390/jcm10010123.

## Chapter 2
1. Indigenous Corporate Training Inc. 2020. "What Is the Seventh Generation Principle?" Accessed 14 August, 2024. https://www.ictinc.ca/blog/seventh-generation-principle.
2. Krockow, Eva M. 2018. "How Many Decisions Do We Make Each Day?" *Psychology Today*. Accessed August 14, 2024. https://www.psychologytoday.com/ca/blog/stretching-theory/201809/how-many-decisions-do-we-make-each-day.
3. McKinsey & Company. 2020. "To Unlock Better Decision Making, Plan Better Meetings." Accessed August 14, 2024. https://www.mckinsey.com/capabilities/people-and-organizational-performance/our-insights/to-unlock-better-decision-making-plan-better-meetings.
4. Pignatiello, Grant A., Richard J. Martin, and Ronald L. Hickman Jr. 2020. "Decision Fatigue: A Conceptual Analysis." *Journal of Health Psychology* 25, no. 1 (March): 123–135. doi.org/10.1177/1359105318763510.
5. Vohs, Kathleen D., Roy F. Baumeister, Brandon J. Schmeichel, Jean M. Twenge, Noelle M. Nelson, and Dianne M. Tice. 2008. "Making Choices Impairs Subsequent Self-Control: A Limited-Resource Account of Decision Making, Self-Regulation, and Active Initiative." *Journal of Personality and Social Psychology* 94, no. 5 (May): 883–898. doi.org/10.1037/0022-3514.94.5.883; Tierney, John. 2011. "Do You Suffer from Decision Fatigue?" *New York Times*. Accessed August 14, 2024. https://www.nytimes.com/2011/08/21/magazine/do-you-suffer-from-decision-fatigue.html.
6. Isobel, Sophie, Andrea McCloughen, Melinda Goodyear, and Kim Foster. 2021. "Intergenerational Trauma and Its Relationship to Mental Health Care: A Qualitative Inquiry." *Community Mental Health Journal* 57, no. 4 (August): 631–643. doi.org/10.1007/s10597-020-00698-1.
7. Albeck, H. J. 1992. "Intergenerational Consequences of Trauma: Refraining Traps in Treatment Theory: A Second Generation Perspective." In *Handbook of*

*Post Traumatic Therapy*, edited by Williams and J. F. Sommer, 106–125. Westport: Greenwood Press.

8  DeAngelis, Tori. 2019. "The Legacy of Trauma: An Emerging Line of Research is Exploring How Historical and Cultural Traumas Affect Survivors' Children for Generations to Come." *Monitor on Psychology* 50, no. 2. https://www.apa.org/monitor/2019/02/legacy-trauma.

9  Braga, Luciana Lorens, Marcelo Feijó Mello, and José Paulo Fiks. 2012. "Transgenerational Transmission of Trauma and Resilience: A Qualitative Study with Brazilian Offspring of Holocaust Survivors." *BMC Psychiatry* 12, no. 134 (September). doi.org/10.1186/1471-244X-12-134.

10  Wolynn, Mark. n.d. "Insights." Accessed August 15, 2024. https://markwolynn.com/insights/.

11  Wolynn, Mark n.d. "Workshops." Accessed August 15, 2024. https://markwolynn.com/workshops/.

12  Stolorow, Robert. 2014. "A Non-Pathologizing Approach to Emotional Trauma." *Psychology Today*. Accessed August 15, 2024. https://www.psychologytoday.com/au/blog/feeling-relating-existing/201412/non-pathologizing-approach-emotional-trauma.

13  Ibid.

14  Zimmerman, Rachel. 2023. "How Does Trauma Spill from One Generation to the Next?" *The Washington Post*. Accessed August 15, 2024. https://www.washingtonpost.com/wellness/2023/06/12/generational-trauma-passed-healing/.

## Chapter 3

1  TRCP Staff. 2011. "It Is Not the Critic Who Counts." *Theodore Roosevelt Conservation Partnership*. Accessed August 15, 2024. https://www.trcp.org/2011/01/18/it-is-not-the-critic-who-counts/.

2  Cherry, Kendra. 2024. "Maslow's Hierarchy of Needs." *Verywell Mind*. Accessed August 15, 2024. https://www.verywellmind.com/what-is-maslows-hierarchy-of-needs-4136760.

3  Maslow, Abraham. 2015. *Toward a Psychology of Being*. Floyd, Virginia: Sublime Books.

4  Daisaku, Ikeda. 1974. "The Flowering of Creative Life Force." *Daisaku Ikeda*. Accessed August 16, 2024. https://www.daisakuikeda.org/main/culture/essays-on-culture/life-force.html.

5  Koschwanez, Heidi E., Ngaire Kerse, Margot Darragh, Paul Jarrett, Roger J. Booth, and Elizabeth Broadbent. 2013. "Expressive Writing and Wound Healing in Older Adults: A Randomized Controlled Trial." *Psychosomatic Medicine* 75, no. 6 (July/August): 581–590. doi.org/10.1097/PSY.0b013e31829b7b2e.

6 Emmons, R. A. and M. E. McCullough. 2003. "Counting Blessings Versus Burdens: An Experimental Investigation of Gratitude and Subjective Well-Being in Daily Life." *Journal of Personality and Social Psychology* 84, no. 2: 377–89. doi.org/10.1037//0022-3514.84.2.377; Iodice, Jo A., John M. Malouff, and Nicola S. Schutte. 2021. "The Association between Gratitude and Depression: A Meta-Analysis." *International Journal of Depression and Anxiety* 4, no. 1. doi.org/10.23937/2643-4059/1710024.

## Chapter 4

1 Altucher, James. 2024. "Ep. 129 - Dr. Wayne Dyer: Namaste." January 3, 2024. 58:55. https://youtu.be/GcbSgdO6MDc.
2 Future Forum. 2023. "Future Forum Pulse." Accessed August 20, 2024. https://futureforum.com/research/future-forum-pulse-winter-2022-2023-snapshot/.
3 Zhao, Xuan and Nicholas Epley. 2022. "Surprisingly Happy to Have Helped: Underestimating Prosociality Creates a Misplaced Barrier to Asking for Help." *Psychological Science* 33, no. 10 (September): 1708–1731. doi.org/10.1177/09567976221097615.
4 Miller, D. T. 1999. "The Norm of Self-Interest." *American Psychologist* 54, no. 12: 1053–1060. doi.org/10.1037/0003-066X.54.12.1053.
5 Larson, Cynthia Sue. n.d. "Quantum Jumps." *RealityShifters*. Accessed August 20, 2024. http://realityshifters.com/pages/quantumjumps.html.
6 Piaget, Jean. 1970. *Psychology and Epistemology: Towards a Theory of Knowledge*. New York: Viking.
7 Mahoney, Michael J. 2003. *Constructive Psychotherapy: A Practical Guide*. New York: Guilford Press.
8 Mahoney, Michael J. and Donald K. Granvold. 2005. "Constructivism and Psychotherapy." *World Psychiatry* 4, no. 2 (June): 74–77. https://www.ncbi.nlm.nih.gov/pmc/articles/PMC1414735/.

## Chapter 5

1 Online Etymology Dictionary. 2022. "Bravery (n.)." Accessed August 21, 2024. https://www.etymonline.com/search?q=bravery.
2 Online Etymology Dictionary. 2021. "Courage (n.)." Accessed August 21, 2024. https://www.etymonline.com/word/courage#etymonline_v_19178.
3 OHCHR. n.d. "What Are Human Rights?" *United Nations*. Accessed August 21, 2024. https://www.ohchr.org/en/what-are-human-rights.
4 Elder, Linda and Richard Paul. 2014. "Becoming a Fairminded Thinker." *Critical Thinking: Tools for Taking Charge of Your Professional and Personal Life*. New Jersey: Pearson.

5   Connell, Sophia M. and Frederique Janssen-Lauret. 2022. "Lost Voices: On Counteracting Exclusion of Women from Histories of Contemporary Philosophy." *British Journal for the History of Philosophy* 30, no. 2 (August): 199–210. doi.org/10.1080/09608788.2021.1984201.

## Chapter 6

1   Weick, Karl E. 1984. "Small Wins: Redefining the Scale of Social Problems." *American Psychologist* 39, no. 1: 40–49. doi.org/10.1037/0003-066X.39.1.40.

2   Brickman, Philip, Donald T. Campbell, and Mortimer H. Appley. 1971. "Adaptation Level Theory: A Symposium." *Hedonic Relativism and Planning the Good Society:* 287-305; Brickman, Philip, Dan Coates, and Ronnie Janoff-Bulman. 1978. "Lottery Winners and Accident Victims: Is Happiness Relative?" *Journal of Personality and Social Psychology* 36, no. 8: 917. doi.org/10.1037//0022-3514.36.8.917; Luhmann, Maike, Wilhelm Hofmann, Michael Eid, and Richard E. Lucas 2012. "Subjective Well-Being and Adaptation to Life Events: A Meta-Analysis." *Journal of Personality and Social Psychology* 102, no. 3: 592–615. doi.org/10.1037/a0025948.

3   Brickman, Philip, Dan Coates, and Ronnie Janoff-Bulman. 1978. "Lottery Winners and Accident Victims: Is Happiness Relative?" *Journal of Personality and Social Psychology* 36, no. 8: 917. doi.org/10.1037//0022-3514.36.8.917.

4   Young, Kyle. 2019. "Harvard Professor Says 'Winning a $20 Million Lottery Won't Make You Happier in Life'—but These 4 Things Will." *CNBC*. Accessed August 22, 2024. https://www.cnbc.com/2019/05/31/harvard-professor-says-winning-20-million-lottery-wont-make-you-happy-but-heres-what-will.html.

5   Mochon, Daniel, Michael I. Norton, and Dan Ariely. 2008. "Getting off the Hedonic Treadmill, One Step at a Time: The impact of Regular Religious Practice and Exercise on Well-Being." *Journal of Economic Psychology* 29, no. 5 (November): 632–642. doi.org/10.1016/j.joep.2007.10.004.

6   Wilber, Ken (@ken.wilber.official). Instagram post. May 3, 2021. https://www.instagram.com/ken.wilber.official/p/COYLVaahile/.

7   Tolle, Eckhart. 2009. *A New Earth: Awakening to Your Life's Purpose*. London: Penguin.

8   Jung, Carl. 2014. *Collected Works of C. G. Jung, Volume 16: Practice of Psychotherapy*. Princeton: Princeton University Press.

## Chapter 7

1   Australian Institute of Health and Welfare. 2024. "People Using Aged Care." *Australian Government*. Accessed August 23, 2024. https://www.gen-agedcaredata.gov.au/topics/people-using-aged-care.

2   Fidan, Özlem, Nesrin Çunkuş Köktaş, and Arife Şanlialp Zeyrek. 2024. "The Relationship between Moral Courage and Lovingkindness-Compassion Levels in Critical Care Nurses: A Cross-Sectional Study." *Australian Critical Care* 37, no. 3 (May): 468–474. doi.org/10.1016/j.aucc.2023.04.009.

3   Cleveland Clinic. 2023. "Caregiver Burnout." Accessed August 26, 2024. https://my.clevelandclinic.org/health/diseases/9225-caregiver-burnout.

4   Ibid.

5   Hunsaker, Stacie, Hsiu-Chin Chen, Dale Maughan, and Sondra Heaston. 2015. "Factors That Influence the Development of Compassion Fatigue, Burnout, and Compassion Satisfaction in Emergency Department Nurses." *Journal of Nursing Scholarship* 47, no. 2 (March): 186–194. doi.org/10.1111/jnu.12122.

6   Honea, Norissa J., RuthAnn Britnall, Barbara Given, Paula Sherwood, Deirdre B. Colao, Susan C. Somers, and Laurel L. Northouse. 2008. "Putting Evidence into Practice: Nursing Assessment and Interventions to Reduce Family Caregiver Strain and Burden." *Clinical Journal of Oncology Nursing* 12, no. 3 (June): 507–516. doi.org/10.1188/08.CJON.507-516.

7   Cherry, Kendra. 2023. "Compassion Fatigue: The Toll of Caring Too Much." *Verywell Mind*. Accessed August 26, 2024. https://www.verywellmind.com/compassion-fatigue-the-toll-of-caring-too-much-7377301.

8   Kayaalp, Alper, Kyle J. Page, and Kathleen M. Rospenda. 2021. "Caregiver Burden, Work-Family Conflict, Family-Work Conflict, and Mental Health of Caregivers: A Mediational Longitudinal Study." *Work and Stress* 35, no. 3 (October): 217–240. doi.org/10.1080/02678373.2020.1832609.

9   Hua, Alice Y., Jenna L. Wells, Casey L. Brown, and Robert W. Levenson. 2021. "Emotional and Cognitive Empathy in Caregivers of People with Neurodegenerative Disease: Relationships with Caregiver Mental Health." *Clinical Psychological Science* 9, no. 3 (March): 449–466. doi.org/10.1177/2167702620974368.

10  Adapted from: Watson, P., Gist, R., Taylor, V., Evlander, E., Leto, F., Martin, R., Vaught, D., Nah, W.P., Westphal, R., & Litz, B (2013). Stress First Aid for Firefighters and Emergency Services Personnel. National Fallen Firefighters Foundation.

## Chapter 8

1   NSW Department of Health. 2009. "Early Pregnancy – When Things Go Wrong." Accessed August 27, 2024. https://www.health.nsw.gov.au/kidsfamilies/MCFhealth/Publications/early-pregnancy-when-things-go-wrong.pdf.

# Notes

www.ingramcontent.com/pod-product-compliance
Lightning Source LLC
Chambersburg PA
CBHW030253100526
44590CB00012B/391